3rd Edition

FRAMED

&

PROFILED

The Legal Lynching of a Black Psychiatrist

A Memoir

Dr. Van Johnson M.D.

ISBN: 979-8-35096-316-8 (print)

AUTHOR: Dr. Van Johnson, M.D.

United States Library of Congress, Copyright Registration Number: TXu 1-873-698

Dr. Van Johnson, M.D.
4333 Nebraska Avenue; B 307
Saint Louis, Missouri, 63118
Cell phone 314-285-8905
Email address: bigsir_blue@yahoo.com

Prologue

Van Johnson

THERE IS AN OLD SAYING, "TRUTH IS SOMETIMES STRANGER than fiction." That phrase aptly applies to my story, the first black psychiatrist to open a practice in Anderson, Indiana. A lot of my white patients affectionately referred to this region as "Klan country."

This story involves an incident that took place well before the age of cell phones, the internet, Instagram, and other advanced modalities of imaging and communications. Prior to this age of advanced technology, there was no objective evidence whereby blacks could prove that the so-called "Official Statement" by police was nothing more than hogwash. Contrary to popular belief, there was never an objective threshold to obtain a criminal conviction against a black person. The court system in the western world exerts white supremacy through a predominantly white jury system that presides over who will be removed from society. Usually, the accusation of a black man itself is enough to remove any presumption of innocence.

White America has always rallied around the defense of the Second Amendment to the U.S. constitution—the right to possess guns to protect their life and property. Conversely, when I defended my life at home, not one conservative pro-Second Amendment group came to my defense or aid in any capacity. I was faced with the stark reality that negroes are not allowed to successfully invoke the Second Amendment against white assailants. What follows is the most sophisticated and diabolical subterfuge of justice in this country's history.

Chapter One

ON JANUARY 22, 1954, I WAS BORN IN PROVIDENCE HOSPITAL, the only issue from the union of Jonathan Melvin Ivy and Barbara Abrams.

My parents were the offspring of Black religious leaders. Jonathan's father was Elder Berry B. Ivy, the administrative superintendent for the southern district of Missouri in the Church of God in Christ (COGIC). Flora, Jonathan's mother, was a national missionary in that religious order. Barbara's father was Deacon Clarence Johnson, Senior, who sat on the board of the Metropolitan Missionary Baptist Church and was the lead baritone in their choir. He was a democratic ward committeeman in the era of patronage politics in Chicago. Odessa, Barbara's mother, was a schoolteacher who chose to be a stay-at-home parent.

Jonathan grew up in the small town of Charleston, located in the boot hill region of Missouri. He had five brothers and four sisters, however, three of the girls died of tuberculosis in their teen years. Thelma was the only surviving sister. John A. was the oldest and only sibling who fought in WWII. Jonathan and his siblings were coming of age during this era of war.

America was a segregated society at that time. Black people and Whites lived in racially segregated areas throughout the country. There were no civil rights for Black people. Black people were governed by Jim Crow laws, which originated in the south after the Reconstruction period. When WWII ended, the Black soldiers returned home from Europe and other theaters of battle and demanded better treatment here in the U.S. Those soldiers united with black labor unions, black church leaders, and black college student spokesmen to demand civil rights and desegregation. They were tired of separate and inferior accommodations in civil society. This movement began in the churches and Black colleges in the south. It spread across the country like wind-driven wildfire. Initially, the white media paid little attention to the protest. As the white backlash progressed in violence, the civil rights movement gained political momentum. It culminated with every news cycle focused on the Black movement. The question of "What to do with the Negro?" dominated Sunday morning talk shows. Thousands of Black people were killed or injured during those white riots through-out the south. Elder Berry decided to send his sons and only daughter to Chicago for their safety.

Barbara was a nineteen-year-old former high school homecoming queen who aspired to be a top model. She grew up in a tight-knit Baptist family of five sisters and four brothers in Chicago's south side. Jonathan and Barbara met as next-door neighbors on the south side of Chicago. However, the differences in their socio-religious backgrounds created its own tensions. As a result of his strict Pentecostal upbringing, he was unaware of the complex cultural nuances of big city life. She was the product of that fast-paced city culture. As a result, he inadvertently made comments that others perceived as insensitive moral judgments; and there were the gaffes that eventually sabotaged their relationship.

Jonathan lacked his father's 'gift of gab,' but he developed the abil-ity to speak and write fluently in Spanish and French. It was a talent that landed him a middle-management position with a major corporation. (His brothers created the Ivy Construction Company. Their company flourished during the period of racial segregation. Ironically, after the passage of the 1964 Civil Rights Act that prompted integration, their company started losing business to white contractors.)

Barbara's family was always involved with some type of group activ-ity. She always invited Jonathan to their events. He attended but was very quiet and appeared preoccupied. Her brothers initiated the conversation and invited him to join them in various activities. He never socialized with them. They had never met a young black man who didn't drink pop, dance, eat sweets, play cards, board games, or participate in any sports. They liked the fact that he did not drink, smoke, or do drugs. They wondered if he had something against their family. He was an introvert with nothing to say! However, Barbara often ignored his unintentional gaffes. But there's always that "last Straw that broke the Camel's back," so to speak. He experienced it on a perfect Saturday evening at her father's home.

Barbara's father was not only known for being a spiffy dresser, but he also hosted great soirees at his home. Odessa greeted the guests as they arrived on that perfect Saturday evening. As a well-connected Chicago democratic ward committeeman, Clarence's guest list included prominent clerics, politicians, and businessmen. Barbara and her sisters dressed up in beautiful cocktail dresses; and they received a lot of attention. Everyone was enjoying the lively event. Clarence did not smoke or drink himself but allowed guests to bring libations.

Barbara was having a fun time with people she had known since childhood. Jonathan did not know anyone outside of Barbara's family. He sauntered near a small group of men who were drinking, trading locker-room banter and off-colored gossip. Strangely, he got upset even though none of their profane ramblings were directed at him in any way. Barbara noticed his change of mood and asked if there was something wrong. He mentioned the off-colored humor and wanted her to leave the party with him. When she refused, there was a loud argument that caught her father's attention.

Clarence summoned them into a room and queried about the dispute. Jonathan complained about the small gathering of drunk men who spouted vulgarities. Clarence told him, "This is my home and those are my guests. You do not live here so feel free to leave at any time." At that point, Barbara realized that she could not marry a man who was that socially brittle. She was in tears when they left the party. The next time he came to her apartment, she handed him the engagement ring and said… "Goodbye!" It was his last gaffe!

Jonathan was gone, but she was now pregnant. At her family meeting, Odessa suggested that she proceed with the wedding for the sake of her future child. Barbara wanted marriage and a family, but her feelings toward Jonathan had changed. "That thin line between love and hate."

She refused to reconsider marriage with him. There were only two options left: have a child out of wedlock with its social stigma or pay the high cost for an illegal abortion. The family tentatively agreed to pay for the abortion. However, that decision was only tentative. Their father made the final decision in all family matters.

Deacon Clarence Johnson Sr. thought that Jonathan was a young man with high morals and integrity but lacked secular nuances because of his strict Pentecostal upbringing. Clarence went out of his way to meet Jonathan's parents at a COGIC convention held in Chicago. He reported that Elder Berry and Flora gave excellent speeches at the convention. Clarence was a church official with conservative values. He could not fathom giving the okay to abort his own grandchild because his daughter didn't go through with a planned wedding. He announced the decision not to fund her abortion. Barbara felt betrayed and accused him and the family of reneging on their promise. The family consoled her with a pledge of unconditional love and support for the anticipated new addition to their family.

Barbara asked Jonathan for money to pay for her abortion, but he refused. He wanted her to forgive him and proceed with their wedding plans. However, her attitude towards him had become recalcitrant. "No! You will always be this pompous and socially rigid man. People are imperfect. If I thought marriage to you could result in joy and fulfillment, I would still be wearing your engagement ring."

At birth, I weighed seven pounds and ten ounces, and Barbara named me after a movie icon of that era. Clarence performed my church baptism. Atty. Clifford and Bunny, his wife, were present at the ceremony. They were close friends with the Johnson family. After the ceremony, Bunny asked to be my babysitter, which gave Barbara a chance to resume her career. There was never an issue of trust because Bunny had known Barbara when she was a child. Bunny agreed to keep me during the day while Barbara worked. Sometimes, I stayed the whole weekend. They set aside a room in their home for my toys and built a playground in the backyard. Their next-door neighbor had three toddlers named Randy,

Andy, and Sandy, whose parents brought them over every afternoon to play with me in the playground.

Clifford was a partner in an all-black Chicago law firm. Bunny was a well-educated socialite from a prominent Chicago family. Unfortunately, she had a medical condition that precluded the possibility of childbirth. Clifford and Bunny held conferences and other events at the home. I was always the topic of conversation during those events. Every year, they took me to the Kentucky Derby. Stuffed horses littered my toy room.

After church services, Bunny and Odessa took turns hosting dinner at each other's home. That gave me a chance to bond with Gwen, Greta, Betty, and Gloria, my maternal aunts, as well as Clarence Jr., Douglas, Richard, and Russell, my uncles, and Clarence Sr. and Odessa, my maternal grandparents.

Bunny wanted to adopt me, but Barbara wouldn't go that far: She allowed them to be my surrogates. Regardless of my legal status, the couple treated me like their child.

Jonathan financially supported Barbara and me very well. Everything was going fine until his mother compelled him to seek joint custody. Jonathan knew about the arrangement Barbara had with Clifford and Bunny and had no problem with it because there was no complaint about their care.

At that time in my life, I had little contact with Flora. It was rumored that she stirred up trouble between Barbara and Jonathan over my care. She and the COGIC presiding Bishop of Chicago were good friends. She was a domineering matriarch with narcissistic traits. My care was really none of Flora's business, but she used her religious connections to get the Illinois Department of Family Services involved in my care. What was Flora's logic for getting involved? Since Jonathan and Barbara did not have the big wedding as planned, she viewed his financial support as a form of alimony and thought it would be good if he had shared custody. But Jonathan was happy with his life as a successful young bachelor. My father did not know a thing about the care of an infant. Could he manage a crying infant at 2 a.m. in the morning? No! Flora was acting out of boredom. She had brainwashed Jonathan. He did not have the balls to stand firm on any conviction.

In Chicago, politics is a blood sport, so to speak…and not for the faint of heart. Anything can be accomplished by a person with money or the right connections. Flora proved that! Enough said. One morning, Barbara and a white DCFS worker made an unannounced visit to Clifford's home. The social worker had a court order that demanded Barbara to make arrangements with Jonathan to share custody of me. The DCFS worker handed Clifford the court order. As he read it, tears streamed down his cheeks. When Bunny walked into the living room, he handed her the letter. She read it and collapsed on the floor in a state of hysteria. The white social worker began to cry and said, "I did not want to do this, but it is my job. Jonathan's family was behind this court action.'" I heard the commotion in the living room but did not know what was going on. Clifford summoned me. I walked in the room and noticed everyone in tears. Bunny held me in her arms and explained that I would be going to live with my father. She asked Barbara, "Why didn't you notify us if there was a problem?" Barbara explained that she had just found out early that morning. As a child, I did not understand the complexity of the matter. However, I knew it was serious because everyone I loved was in tears! Clifford and Bunny were as much of my family as the Johnsons. They cared for me throughout infancy and the formative years of childhood. I spent little time around my father and did not know his family.

I sat on the sofa and watched Bunny pack my clothes, toys, and stuffed animals in luggage and tote bags. Clifford helped me into my overcoat, and then everyone went on the front porch. Clifford and Bunny remained on the porch sobbing and watched Barbara and the social worker load my belongings into a car trunk. The social worker was the driver. Barbara sat next to me in the back seat. As the car pulled away from the curb, I turned around and saw my surrogates wailing and waving goodbye through the back window. Once I moved in with Jonathan, I often thought about Clifford, Bunny, Randy, Andy, and Sandy. I never saw them again. Barbara never took me again to that Baptist church, or to Odessa's home on Sunday evenings. One of my first lessons in life was the impermanence of people, places, and things.

We arrived at Barbara's apartment. A tall, well-dressed man appeared uncomfortable on the living room sofa. Jonathan arrived that evening and took me to a three-bedroom apartment he shared with his sister Thelma, her white husband, and their two sons. (In the 1950s, a white man living in the Black community was an anomaly.) I knew it would be a difficult adjustment living with my father. It was my first encounter with a white man. He was a short well-built man who seemed angry and kept tension in the air. He pitted his children against me in every way possible. My aunt Thelma married him because she was obsessed with having "light-skinned children." In Black society, skin shade has always had just as much influence as education or money. As proof, calling a Negro "Black" in the 1950s-60s could've got you a beat-down, or killed. Some black leaders and musicians tried to counterpro-gram this sickness. For example, in 1964, James Brown produced the record *I'm Black and I'm Proud*. Rev. Jesse Jackson had audiences repeat the mantra, "I am Black, I am somebody." Elijah Muhammad, leader of the Nation of Islam, authored the book *Message to the Blackman in America*.

I became accustomed to the services of the Baptist church: Sunday services were at 11:00 a.m. and 1:00 p.m. Each usually went for an hour. I was used to hearing members of the congregation being introduced as doctor, attorney, etc. The service was brief and to the point. Socialization took place at each other's homes after church services.

Now, I had to attend a Church of God in Christ (COGIC). It meant 8:30 a.m. services to start the morning. Then, continuous services throughout the day. There were lunch and dinner breaks. The last service ended at 9:00 p.m. The congregation was socially conservative. Most women wore dark dresses below their knees, blouses did not expose shoul-ders, and no high heel shoes. The women never wore pant suits or form-fitting garments. Men wore dark suits, white shirts, and black shoes.

The deacons kept the order in the church. If you screwed up, you got your ass beat…period! The congregation gave them permission to whoop any child's ass, if necessary. Every Sunday, a women's committee prepared the evening dinner for the congregation. In that day, there were very few fast-food outlets. Those group dinners kept the flock together. Young males are hyperactive and often get bored sitting for long periods of time. To combat this, they gave us something to do—manually prepare cylinders of homemade ice cream in the church basement. A group of us took turns spinning a large cylinder of liquid ice cream surrounded by ice chips covered with salt. While the congregation was listening to sermons, we were downstairs playing the dozens–things boys learn early in life. In between turning that cylinder, we played with our yo-yos, traded vulgarities, and had fist fights. One Sunday, a fight erupted over a comment about someone's sister. Mr. Sims, the head deacon, appeared out of nowhere holding a leather belt, "They can hear that loud cursing upstairs. Where did you boys learn that language?" He whooped everyone's ass. Not one parent ever thought about calling the sheriff, or police.

The all-day sermons had a consistent theme—fear of strangers, death, the Devil, and God. The most interesting phenomenon is what I called "the 6 p.m. happy hour." This peculiar service began with an inspirational speech by the pastor's wife. Then, one by one, people stood up and testified about how God blessed them. Usually, their testimony is accompanied by shouting, crying, erratic dancing, or so-called speaking in tongues. It was like the Catholic confessional, except that it was on display for all to see and hear. I thought it was the best service of all because there were members of the congregation expressing real emotion and feelings.

When I reached fourteen, it was no longer mandatory for me to attend church services. It elated me to have that option. I never attended church services again until my older years.

When Jonathan purchased a large home, Thelma agreed to be my caretaker in exchange for living there rent-free with her family. The Offord's had their section in the home. I always had my own bedroom. Visiting guests stayed in the apartment downstairs. We used the basement as a skating rink. There was a large backyard with a pear tree. It was never used for anything. I wondered if it had something to do with their religious beliefs.

When I started taking private piano lessons from the music director at church, Jonathan purchased a piano for me to practice my lessons at home. It was not long before my uncle-in-law started "player-hating." Whenever I began practice sessions, he banged on my door to complain about the noise. He would verbally abuse me when Joe was not around. I did not understand why he married a black woman. He often referred to blacks as savages. Jonathan got fed up with his turmoil and canceled my piano lessons. I was just a child trying to grow up in a Jim Crow household.

The stress in that home may have been the cause of my sudden onset of asthma attacks around the age of six. The adults viewed my suffering with indifference. One evening during a severe attack, I gasped for air as my saved-and-sanctified aunt Thelma placed a sheet over my body without bothering to call an ambulance. Sometimes, the attacks were so severe I'd stay up all night and read encyclopedias to divert my attention from that agonizing medical condition.

My father finally took me to a black medical doctor named Dr. K. Wallace, MD. His wife was a nurse and ran the office. After a complete physical exam, he asked Joe, "Are you aware that those attacks could kill your child?" Dr. Wallace prescribed theophylline tablets and a "rescue inhaler" for acute attacks. He remarked that I was a highly intelligent child and asked Joe if I could do small chores at the clinic after school. I accepted the doctor's offer. My job was to empty the small trash cans throughout the clinic. The doctor had to have another reason for me being there because those trash cans rarely contained any refuse. The patients in the waiting room were curious about me and asked questions about my background. They were friendly and often engaged me in small talk. Some patients thought that I was the doctor's son. I often loitered near an examination room where he was performing a procedure on someone. I watched the doctor perform procedures on patients.

Dr. Wallace had a private office with a library and other things that stimulated my mind. I would sneak in and browse through his medical textbooks, fascinated by the color photos of diseased organs and tissue. Once, I climbed on his leather chair to get on the desk and look through the microscope. He quietly walked in and caught me in the act. He just smiled and asked if I saw anything interesting in the books. I will never forget the time when I was in the X-ray department staring at some X-ray films on a panel. Dr. Wallace walked in, grabbed a seat, and asked me to describe what was happening on the X-rays. When I pointed at them, we both broke out laughing. He never got angry at my curiosity and drove me home after work every day.

I joined the cub scout den near my home. Their meetings were held in a Baptist church. We played all sorts of games with carving projects. James Alexander III was one of my elementary school classmates in that den. We were the same age, height, and weight. He lived down the street from me in a Spanish-style Villa. Their backyard had a white five-foot picket fence. He had a mean German Shepard named Sandy. His mother was the first Black female vice-president for Bell Telephone company. His father was a civil engineer that worked in the downtown federal building. James and I walked to and from elementary school together. We eventually joined the same Boy Scout and Civil Air Patrol units.

In fifth grade, when I entered a project at the science fair, James was my assistant. I won the first-place prize. The next year, I entered another project, and it also won the first-place prize. I showed Dr. Wallace my certificates. He smiled and said, "I'm not surprised."

The Rivieras were the only Mexican family in our neighborhood. Franky, their oldest boy, started a little league baseball team called the Dragons. I was a starting pitcher and James played left field on the team. It was a lot of fun. There is nothing like a large crowd of adults watching us compete on a warm summer evening. For me, it was all about getting out of that house.

James and I decided to make some money washing cars. We got the idea from watching the adults dress up to go out on Friday and Saturday evenings. We purchased large sponges and a liquid cleaner called "Rain Dance" made by the Johnson and Johnson company. We solicited every homeowner on respective blocks. The adults smiled at us for charging only $1.00 per car. But we did a great job! The homeowners had only to hook up their garden hose to the water supply so that we could rinse off the soap. Everyone hired us out. We operated as a team. Each of us washed half of the vehicle. Then we towel dried them. Instead of giving us $1.00, most customers handed us a $5 dollar bill, and told us to keep the change! That was a large amount of money for a kid in the early 1960s. By the end of summer, I had opened a savings account with a passbook containing $300 dollars. Yes, banks gave passbooks back then. We successfully did it for two summers and made enough money to purchase our favorite junk foods—turtle candy, cheese-and-crackers, and ginger cookies.

Every summer, we took the train to Charleston, Missouri. It was Thelma and Jonathan's birthplace. We went there to spend time with our grandparents—to kiss their rings, is more like it. It was a journey to the segregated south, which called for Thelma getting up early to prepare snacks for the long train ride south. Usually, she cooked fried chicken, salami sandwiches, potato salad, and cake or pie. Traveling by train was popular in the 1950s. However, Black people were not allowed into the train's Club Cars. So, they brought their own food. The last two train cars were for blacks only.

Once the passengers were settled into their seats, the conversations commenced like old friends. The children would find a place to congregate and play games. A small number of men congregated at the back of the last car to drink, smoke, play cards, and shoot dice. Midway through the trip, Thelma passed out the food. This prompted other families to do the same.

It took about three to four hours to reach Cairo, Illinois. Berry and Flora would be waiting for us at the end of the platform. Since they both drove Cadillac's, we split up into two groups. I loved the scenic greenery of farms and pastures during those summer trips. My grandfather often took us fishing. He would behead and gut the fish on a table in the backyard. Two cats watched the ritual perched on top of the fence. He would throw them the fish parts after he finished.

Berry's sermons were pure "Fire and Brimstone". He had everybody going to hell, including the pets, so to speak. Many years later, I found out that he often stated that Black people were a cursed people! I heard that white folks considered him and Flora, the most outstanding black couple in town. In 1965, Elder Berry passed away. His body lay in state at city hall for two days.

One thing I came to understand over the years is that the Church is the most influential and wealthiest institution in the Black community. As a national missionary, many in the religious community referred to my grandmother as the "Adept". They held revivals under Billy Graham-styled large tents. Hundreds of people attended those gatherings Thursday through Saturday evenings. As we kids grew older, the duration and frequency of those visits decreased. From middle school through high school, I did not make the trip back down south. The last time I went to Charleston was during my summer break between the first year and second year of medical school. I brought lots of books with me to study. One day for lunch, Flora and I went to a nearby town called Sikeston. It was our first and last one-on-one! She started the conversation with the concept of conversion to Christianity. I was shocked when she mentioned her wish that I had obtained a Doctor of Divinity degree from Mason University in Memphis, Tn. It is the national flagship of the Church of God in Christ. Then she got deep. "Van, did you ever think about being the pastor of a large church?' In the religious community, you would be highly revered and make the same or more money than in the field of medicine. You would meet a saved, well-educated black woman who would be an ideal wife to bring forth your next generation. The white people at that all-white medical school you attend, view you as a threat. They will limit your future in their world." I was impressed with her wisdom. It also helped me understand why years later, she didn't attend my medical school graduation.

Jonathan and I never had a close relationship. I could remember only once when he took me to Riverview, Chicago's largest amusement park in the 1950s. My father never passed down any family history. What little I learned came from my great aunt Lottie. Jonathan took care of me out of guilt, and to impress his mother. As a man caring for a small child, he became the prize catch in the eyes of the single women in our church congregation. During his absences from home, I was left alone to deal with the vitriol that came from my white uncle-in-law.

In 1968, I was in the eighth grade and set to graduate from middle school. Chicago had one of the most segregated school systems in the country. A lawsuit to desegregate its school system had lingered in the federal court for years. However, after the assassination of Dr. Martin Luther King, Jr. in April 1968, the federal court mandated integration of the schools. White America was responding to Black people rioting in over one hundred cities across the country. The country was on the verge of an all-out race war! White America enacted emergency legislation to integrate every aspect of civil society. They called it Affirmative Action. The Chicago Board of Education chose to desegregate its school system through a permissive transfer program. Black students with promise or high IQs could now apply for entry into historically all-white high schools on the city's north and far southwest sides. (This explained why everyone in my eighth-grade class had to take an IQ test!)

James and I applied to the Von Steuben Science center. They accepted both of us. Our lives were on a parallel course. We were partners who won two science fairs, members of the same Cub Scout and Boy scout dens, and members of the same Civil Air Patrol unit. We both joined the same beginners' band in middle school. He chose to master the cornet; I chose the French horn. Now, we were both going to attend the same high school. The Von Steuben science center is located on the far north side of Chicago. It sits on a tributary of the Chicago River next to North Park University. The faculty and student body were Jewish. All the instructors had graduate degrees. Mel Brown was the only Black teacher there when I started. She holds a master's degree. They utilized her as a counselor and liaison to the black students, which made up less than two percent of the student body. The predominantly Jewish student body consisted of the arrogant progeny of judges, doctors, lawyers, and wall street executives.

On our first day of class, the black students were summoned into the assembly hall. Dr. Lubov, the principal, said that it took a community referendum for us to be allowed into their pristine community. "It's a privilege for all of you to attend a high school adjacent to a college campus," he said. Dr. Lubov concluded his message by presenting their code of conduct, or more aptly their "Riot Act." "We will not tolerate any gang activity, fighting, graffiti, insubordination, profanity, tardiness, drug or alcohol use. Those infractions will result in your immediate expulsion from this school!"

The black students held a meeting for their own safety in that area of town. When school let out for the day, we, the males, made sure that every black student safely caught the bus or El train home. The segregated South had their sundown towns. Towns where blacks had to be out by sundown lest they face violence or death. Chicago had sundown neighborhoods in the city. Only the schools had recently been integrated.

The white students elected me president of the class. I did not understand why because they had just met me days earlier. Additionally, I did not know how to execute the power of that position, which was in name only. The white students made up whatever rules they wanted and told me afterward.

James and I were immediately accepted into the concert band and began practicing with the band within weeks.

I could not focus on academics because of my complicated home life. The tension between my uncle-in-law and myself progressively worsened as I got taller in height. I was over six feet tall upon entering high school. I wondered if he felt threatened. I worked part time to purchase nice outfits and maintain my "Jerri curl." I was just as lost as any other teenager but took joy in wearing a tailor-made tuxedo to my junior and senior proms.

Jonathan was more distracted now that he became engaged to a young schoolteacher in our church congregation. We became more distant, and there was never any closeness. Jessie, his fiancée, and I never had a conversation during her courtship with my father. I did not understand because I spent time together with her younger brothers in the church. Jonathan started treating me like a stranger. He did not purchase the suit I wanted to wear to his wedding, so I did not attend the event. The family, neighbors, and church congregation were shocked at my absence. Many of my high school classmates attended his wedding. (Jonathan was president of the block club and had invited our neighbors.)

I told Barbara about his engagement and weird ass behavior towards me. She was not surprised and opined, "It is that type of pompous social gaffe that drove me away from him. That's why I didn't marry him."

When I arrived at Von Steuben on Monday morning, the classmates who attended my father's wedding told everyone about my absence from that event. It spread like wildfire throughout the student body. A few white students were bold enough to ask if the rumor was true. I confirmed it. Mel Brown, the black counselor, had me come to her office. She asked why I did not attend my father's wedding. I explained that our relationship was purely financial in nature. She appeared deeply saddened by that revelation. I believe that as a black woman, she not only understood my situation but has witnessed a lot of "Social Garbage" in the black community.

After his big wedding, Joe bought a new home and gave Thelma the home we lived in. He gave me a one-bedroom apartment with a weekly allowance. I was sixteen years old with the freedom of an adult, without the bills. It was my responsibility to construct a lifestyle. I had an athletic built at six feet two inches tall, which is why my father never worried about my safety. I finally got the much-needed separation from my uncle-in-law and his children. I did not hang out with thugs or other low-bred trash, drink or do drugs. The few friends I had were musicians like me. We spent time collecting, exchanging, and sampling record albums. I had a voluminous collection of recorded albums by artists of every genre.

I started dating older women, i.e., twenty and thirty-year-olds because most of them had apartments or homes, and steady jobs. They provided me with cheer over the long winter holidays. With no curfew or travel restrictions, I worked part-time at several grocery stores, and obtained a Longshoreman's union card to work on the Navy pier docks. I lied about my age to get a busser job at the Playboy Club, located in downtown Chicago at 119 E. Walton St. If I did not have to work, why did I get those jobs? I wanted to impress my black classmates. I spent my money on the latest knit sweaters and shoes from Smokey Joe's in Jewtown. But working at the Playboy was the ultimate exciting job for a teenager. I spend my evenings around attractive, scantily clad women in Bunny outfits; watching rich white men get drunk and brag about their buildings, boats, planes, and companies. Hugh Hefner, Playboy's founder, made a visit one evening wearing a dark shirt with a maroon smoking jacket and surrounded by bodyguards. He waved at the guests, then left.

I went directly to school after working my shift. The subway station was half a block from the club. I would often fall asleep during those long train rides to the far north side. The job started taking a toll on me, and I began falling asleep in some classes. One instructor was overly concerned about this unusual conduct from me. The counselor had me come to her office and asked if I was on drugs or drinking alcohol. I came clean and told Mel about the night job at the Playboy club. She laughed her ass off. "'How did you get that job?'" You are only sixteen, going on seventeen years old," she asked. I told her that I lied about my age. She just shook her head and gave me an ultimatum, "You either quit that job or get expelled from this school!" I loved the nightlife at the club and did not want to quit that job. I got myself fired a week later for attempting to steal a Bunny's tip—the first time I ever attempted to steal something.

The faculty viewed my lack of interest in academics as adolescent "growing pains." They knew that I had potential and a high IQ, more than I did. Dr. Samuel Bromberg, my math instructor, took a special interest in me. He offered to tutor me in math after school. I accepted that offer. However, at the start, I told him that I wanted to play basketball in the NBA and was not interested in academics. Dr. Bromberg laughed. "Van, I have seen you play. Your game sucks! Statistically, you have a better chance of becoming a doctor or lawyer." After months of tutoring, I was getting the top scores in his math class. The other students in the class were shocked. My lackadaisical ass was now beating them. In my senior year, I kicked ass in the Advanced Placement courses in college algebra, trigonometry, and pre-calculus.

Despite my marginal academic performance, I maintained a stellar consistency in two areas: The concert band and chess club. I worked my way up to sharing the first chair in the concert band during my last year. They placed me in the concert band when I entered Von Steuben. As a senior, I was better than Sue Solomon, my competitor. However, Mr. Zayda, the band director, made us share the first chair music, which meant more solo performances. I believe his motivation for doing this was political: Sue Solomon's father was a federal judge. There's nothing more exciting than performing very well and receiving that long ovation from the crowd. I can feel the adrenaline that rock stars experience. That's the power of music!

In late spring 1970, the teachers announced in every class that James Alexander III had been shot over the weekend. He was now in the intensive care unit. Two white police officers were patrolling his neighborhood. From over a hundred feet away, they saw a Black teen wrestling with a large German Shepard in a backyard of an ornate home. Despite no radio traffic of a burglary, they thought the teen was a burglar and shot him with a high-powered rifle! (Before Affirmative Action, most urban police departments were comprised of all-white male police officers.) At Von Steuben, the faculty and student body held a prayer service for James. I had never seen so many white people in tears for a black teen.

Jonathan knew James well. Whenever we had to play in a concert, James came by my home with his horn. We would depart together, horns in hand. I told Joe what happened to James. He held his head down and wept. Until that moment, I never thought my father had any feelings. We paid a visit to my friend's home. Mrs. Alexander was in deep grief. Her phone was constantly ringing so we kept the visit brief. We left, but I returned several days later. Mrs. Alexander could not understand why her son was gunned down in his own backyard. She mentioned that he was in the ICU and had undergone major surgeries. I went into a deep despair. We had experienced so much together. He was like the brother I never had.

I was the first and only Black person on the school's chess team, which was considered a sport, despite its non-contact nature. In those days, the school system barred women from participating in sports activities. When they allowed me on the team as the first black person, it prompted a white female Jewish student to file a discrimination lawsuit against the Chicago Board of Education and Von Steuben. We did not know about her lawsuit until they notified us that a news station would be doing a segment on her story. One day, as we were having matches in a classroom, a Channel 7 T.V. crew walked in and filmed us. I saw myself on the 5 p.m. and 10 p.m. news. I believed the only reason she filed that lawsuit was that they allowed me on the team. As I watched the news segment about her suit, I noticed how they focused the camera on me, amid my white male classmates. There was no audio taping with the story.

In my senior year of prep school, I got tired of classmates discussing their college ambitions. Several classmates received early admission into Dartmouth and M.I.T., some prestigious schools. The students had a ritual that whenever someone received an acceptance letter to college, there was a public announcement made in the cafeteria. The student body gave them a standing ovation. I had no ambition and did not care about anything beyond high school. My instructors and Mel Brown continued to badger me every day about some type of plan.

But things changed, and so did I. It happened during a weekend trip to a flea market called Jewtown. It is located on Maxwell Street, one block south of the University of Illinois Chicago (UIC). I fell in love with the panoramic view of the downtown skyline. As the Halsted Street bus cruised through the campus, I intuitively knew that my destiny would be at that institution.

On Monday morning, I asked Mel to research my chances of getting into the UIC. She relayed my interest to the entire faculty. They researched the school's admission criteria and gave me some unwelcome news. My English and Social Studies scores on the ACT and SAT were too low for acceptance into the college of Liberal Arts and Sciences (LAS). The College of Engineering was the only other option because of my math and science scores.

In April 1972, I received a letter from the college of engineering at the University of Illinois, Chicago. In anticipation of sad news, I gave the letter to Dr. Pollack, an assistant principal with a reputation for brute sarcasm. He read the letter and said that I had been accepted into the college of engineering. He came around the desk and gave me a hug. "Van, you have another chance to start fresh. Please, do not fuck up this opportunity." He took me to the faculty lounge, held up my acceptance letter, and announced that I had been accepted into the University of Illinois. The faculty gave me a standing ovation. The next morning, I received a standing ovation at breakfast from my classmates. But it was nothing compared to my eight classmates accepted into Ivy League schools. In addition, three were accepted into the University of Chicago, one into UC Berkeley, and another into Stanford. Every classmate got into a college of some type. A Greek classmate was accepted into the Culinary Institute of America in New York. His family owned a chain of restaurants and he wanted to become a chef.

Jonathan read my college acceptance letter. He said I could keep the apartment and continue to receive an allowance under one condition—I had to stay in school and make something of myself.

In the fall of 1972, I began taking the core required courses in engineering. After several weeks, I realized that engineering was not my calling. I wanted to transfer to the College of Liberal Arts and Sciences (LAS) and major in biology. This involved an interview with the dean of that college. During my meeting with Dean Corbally, he asked why I wanted to transfer to LAS. I told him my plan to graduate in three years with a major in biology and enter medical school. He stared at me and turned every color in the rainbow, so to speak. Corbally mentioned the fact that my low scores on the SAT and ACT prevented my acceptance into the LAS college directly from high school. He surprised me by saying that I was now playing the game correctly and granted my request for transfer.

I took a full load of classes after entering the college of LAS and simultaneously enrolled in evening courses at the Malcolm X community college, which was only half a mile away. The two schools had dual enrollment programs with transferable credits. At Malcolm X, I took the core requisite courses in English composition and other requirements. It provided me with a social balance in contrast to the all-white UIC milieu. They hosted seminars by nationally known Black scholars and leaders from all disciplines. There were free music concerts by well-known black musicians, and African art exhibitions. I would arrive early for classes, which gave me time for some chess and to scope the gorgeous "Sista's."

In 1973, I was studying in UIC's Montgomery room. A young Black man stood out in the sea of white students who normally studied there. He looked familiar. I got up and walked over to introduce myself. I sat next to him and asked if we had ever met. He said, "You are Van. Do you remember James Alexander?" We hugged. I could not believe my eyes. He explained that police had shot him in the lower spine, and he spent over six months in the hospital ICU. After being transferred out of the ICU, he underwent several years of rehabilitation to learn to walk again. While in the hospital, the teachers from Von Steuben brought him study material and all types of gifts and food on weekends. His parents filed a multi-million dollar civil suit against the police who shot him. Nothing happened to the culprits; however, the court awarded his family 6.5 million dollars in the civil suit. He was permanently damaged in an area I will not reveal. I was happy that he was alive and well, and not bound to a wheelchair.

During an evening course in human anatomy and physiology, the instructor offered me a part-time job as a dental assistant. He was Dr. Clarence Edmund Burton, the first Black graduate of Loyola's dental school. He had a busy private practice and taught part-time. I received the highest score in his class and needed the type of work experience he offered on my resume.

The Community Dental Clinic was the name of Dr. Burton's private practice. The clinic was in the heart of the black community. They treated an average of thirty-six patients every day. It took a while for me to get accustomed to certain protocols. However, within a year, my performance had progressed to the level of a certified dental hygienist. After several years, Dr. Burton allowed me to reshape the anatomy of class 1 and class 2 amalgam fillings. I don't think that any white dentists would've given a nineteen-year-old black teen that type of opportunity.

Mandi was the office manager and a licensed dental hygienist. She brought her cousin Cynthia to Chicago from Louisiana—an eighteen-year-old, drop-dead beauty! They were going to train her to be a dental assistant. Cynthia and I hit it off from the very start. We started dating and became nearly inseparable. The other women were happy to see a young handsome couple. They thought we were a perfect match. However, I had to deal with the jealousy and envy of other males at the clinic. They had their eyes on her as well.

In 1973, a Newsweek article highlighted a pre-med fellowship at Harvard University. Curiosity led me to obtain an application. I returned it and completely forgot about the matter. I calculated that acceptance to Harvard was akin to the odds of winning the lottery—next to impossible!

In the Spring of 1974, I stopped by Barbara's home to check on her. She told me that the mail carrier delivered a certified letter from Harvard University. However, only I could sign the letter. She gave me the location of the nearest post office. I went there and signed my letter. I opened it and read it right there at the counter. The news made me nearly faint in the lobby. "Dear Van Johnson, you have been accepted to the Harvard Health Careers Program. Please complete the enclosed forms and return them within a week." I stood there in a state of shock. Being accepted to America's most prestigious university was beyond my belief. I showed the acceptance letter to Dean Corbally of LAS. He blushed but did not say anything. My instructors, classmates, and friends were elated at my good news. I became somewhat of a celebrity on campus.

Everyone at the dental clinic was happy for my success. Cynthia and I went to make copies of the letter and got quite romantic. Mandi walked by and saw us. She advised us to get a hotel room after work. We laughed! Dr. Burton was so elated, he rescheduled patients, closed the clinic early, and took the staff to dinner at the Playboy club. As our entourage was being escorted into the dining area, I had flashbacks of working there as a busser in high school.

On the morning of my scheduled flight to Boston, Cynthia went with me to the airport. She was by my side until I boarded the plane. When I arrived at Boston's Logan airport, a team from Harvard was waiting to transport me and other arriving students to the campus. When we arrived on campus, a faculty assistant led everyone to an area in front of Matthews Hall, located in Harvard yard. Dr. Bill Wallace was the director of the fellowship program. He was a folk hero in the Boston area: a star athlete who nearly died from a football injury in college. He was the first Black man in history to receive a Ph.D. in Botany from Harvard. Dr. Wallace insisted on us calling him Bill. He gave us a short speech on our purpose for being on campus. His assistant assigned everyone to an advisor and tutor. Then we received our IDs and room assignments in the dorms in Harvard Yard. That evening, our first meal in the dining hall was noteworthy. The hall had oak paneled walls lined with oil portraits of wealthy white male benefactors. There were four different menus. A student had to get back in line for seconds.

My advisor was Dr. Clarence Smith, IV, a Florida native who graduated from Harvard College, and matriculated at Tufts medical school. He completed his residency and a hematology fellowship at Massachusetts General Hospital and lived in the affluent suburb of Brookline. Every weekend, I went to his fancy apartment to party and meet his Harvard-educated peers.

They assigned me to room 40 in Weld Hall. (President John F. Kennedy resided there as a student.) The dorm was organized into four-room quads. I shared the quad with a Black student from San Diego that planned to be a gynecologist; a Hispanic student from New York who attended Fordham University in New York; and a Cuban that attended the University of Miami, in Florida. After we left the dorm for classes, a housekeeping crew made up our beds, swept and mopped the common area; cleaned the restroom. Harvard recruited their housekeeping staff from a nearby housing project.

I took a class in cell biology and immunology. There were fourteen students in the class -- far smaller class size than an average university.

Harvard's reputation for academic rigor was not a myth. Our study group often went to bed after midnight.

The staff planned outings, soirées, and a talent show. A group of us toured The Oceanic Institute, an elite research center, at Woods Hole, MA. The staff took us into a lab where they were conducting experiments on gigantic electric eels. There were many areas in the facility that were off-limits to us. They were conducting classified research for the department of defense. We were introduced to an old hippie-looking white guy with a pipe in his mouth. He had won the Nobel prize in Medicine for mapping the Retina of the human eye. Wow! We had a ball at this research facility. After the tour, we went to a nearby public beach on the Atlantic coast. It was adjacent to a long row of oceanfront mansions; each with its private slice of the Atlantic Ocean. As we were enjoying the view, a small world war1 biplane flew parallel to the coastline. It was the only thing in the calm clear skies. Out of nowhere, a casually dressed police officer approached the group. He reminded us not to trespass on the adjacent private properties.

Of course, all fairytales come to an end. On our last morning, we all huddled together and exchanged phone numbers, hugs, and goodbyes in Harvard Yard. There were a lot of tears. We enjoyed getting our asses kicked academically in this pristine world of refinement. On this morning, Dr. Wallace was in rare form. He and the staff watched and formed opinions about us. After congratulating everyone, he began signifying at some of the students, and he played the dozens with others. Bill could talk plenty of cash shit like nobody's business. He had a talent for sniffing out character flaws in people. Nevertheless, most students loved him, and so did I. The real deal behind being accepted to this program: participants had a one-hundred-percent acceptance rate of getting into medical, dental, podiatry, or chiropractic school. Suddenly, a caravan of yellow cabs rolled into "The Yard." We loaded up our belongings for that trip back to the real world.

When I arrived home, it deeply hurt and disappointed me to learn that Cynthia had moved back to Louisiana. Mandi gave me her phone number. Cynthia explained that she got fed up with the continued sexual harassment by the males at the clinic. She was taking courses to complete the requirements to enter nursing school. We both had to keep it moving. I am happy that we shared a lot of time together. We separated on good terms.

In April 1975, I told my father that I would be graduating a year early from college. Jonathan was indifferent and did not say anything. It was a stressful period because I did not know where I'd end up. Dr. Bill Wallace called me from Harvard and said that someone from Rush Medical College spoke with him about me. He said that Rush was going to accept me into their program. Several weeks after his call, I received an acceptance letter from Rush. I told my father, he put his head down and walked away. Most parents would have jumped for joy to have their twenty-one-year-old son accepted into medical school. I was under the misconception that he really wanted me to make something of myself.

In May 1975, I came home nine days before graduation, and everything seemed normal until I had to use the washroom. Someone had nailed wood planks across the door to prevent entry. After I opened it with a neighbor's tools, the face bowl, toilet, and bathtub had been removed. When I notified my father, he claimed no knowledge of the matter. Several days later, he said his wife's brother removed the items, then said, "You got accepted into med school and will survive." My stepmother had several brothers my age, but none of them were on my path. Her oldest brother was Pastor Charles Hughes, a highly decorated Green Beret who owned a two-million-dollar church. I did not understand why he tampered with my living space. Without a washroom, I had to take showers at the Greyhound bus station, or in my college's athletic department. I bought a large bowl to relieve myself at night and had to stop hosting guests.

In June 1975, I graduated from the University of Illinois Chicago after three years, as planned. It was a monumental feat for me. The graduation ceremony took place at the old Chicago stadium on Madison street. Barbara, Thelma, and her husband attended the ceremony. Flora and Joe did not attend. Joe's excuse, "I had to go grocery shopping with my wife."

In the fall of 1975, I was twenty-one years old, and began the curriculum at Rush—one of the youngest in that school's history. To be honest, I felt outdone by the competition. There were only six Black students in my class of 157 students. I was the youngest black student. The majority were light-skinned, older, had at least a master's degree from a white University, or graduated from an Ivy League school. The school boasted of having four Harvard fellows, including me. It was a very alienating experience because you never met a friend, just competitors. Additionally, I will admit that I was immature with some deep shit to process. "Why did my father betray me at such a crucial stage of development?" I needed his financial support more than ever.

To give you a deeper view of the milieu at Rush, consider this. In 1983, Rush kicked out an entire graduating class of Black students—twelve in all. The Black lawyer they retained in a class action suit was allegedly paid $25,000 in cash to blow the case. I saw him several times at the Alpha frat house in Chicago. Most black lawyers will sell out their kind in a heartbeat.

In med school, I completed clerkships at Mount Sinai Hospital of Chicago. It was an excellent facility. I rotated through their pathology department with an interest in forensic pathology. I had no idea whatsoever what the hell I wanted to specialize in after med school! Dr. Rubenstone, the department chair, frowned at my indecisiveness but allowed me to complete an internship in pathology—the backbone of medicine. Dr. William Thomas Jr., the black Co-Chairman of the department, spent a lot of time preparing me for Grand Round presentations. After completing that internship, I entered a family practice internship at Jackson Park Hospital (JPH).

At JPH, a whole new world of opportunities opened for me. At the time, I was taking public transportation from Oak Park to the hospital, a ninety-minute trip. Dr. Leo Beck got tired of my tardiness and offered me an apartment in the Flamingo, a twenty-two-story building he owned on the lakefront in Hyde Park. The apartment had a panoramic view of the crowded lakefront beaches, the traffic on the lakeshore drive, and the steel plants in Gary, Indiana. By bus, it took fifteen minutes to reach the hospital. Living at the Point, the gold coast of the southside, was pure ecstasy. Next door was TJ's five-star restaurant.

I loved the hospital because most of the doctors on staff were Black, Africans, Jews, and a few Asians. Most of the nurses and other support staff were black. I learned more at that hospital than any other. The black attending physicians made every effort to teach you what you needed to know.

I met Diane Preacely as she was coming out of a Chinese laundry on 55th street in Hyde Park. We exchanged numbers and started dating. She had been a writer for Chicago Metro News, Chicago Crusader, Chicago Defender, and the City of Chicago News Bureau newspapers. A publicist at WLS-TV under the acclaimed Irv Kupcinet, who published "Kup's Column" in the Chicago Tribune. In the early 1980's, she was a republican candidate for the U.S. Congress in Chicago's first district. Her photo with a political ad appeared on the giant billboard at 53rd and Lake Park Ave. She was a Jet Magazine centerfold, and a Chicago Policewoman.

We had a whirlwind affair that culminated in a society wedding. Our achievements were featured in a segment of the Chicago Defender newspaper called "Star Galaxy," produced by Earl Calloway. It featured Diane in a half-page photo. She was photogenic! I received my full proper's – Harvard and all. We had a full Catholic mass for a wedding. It was officiated by Father Clements at Holy Angels Church. Our reception was held at the Hyde Park residence of Honorable Elijah Muhammad, founder of The Nation of Islam. Our wedding and reception photos appeared in nine Chicago newspapers.

After passing the FLEX (Federal Licensure Examination) exam, I received my medical license. Dr. Jasper Williams, an Ob/Gyn at JPH, offered me a job at the Williams clinic. It was owned by three brothers and their mother—Dr. Jasper Williams, Jr, Dr. James Williams, and Dr. Charles Williams. Dr. Jasper was a business genius: He had an MBA degree and was also Chairman of the Board of Seaway National

Bank (The largest black bank in America at that time). He owned two television stations, one in Rhinelander, Wisconsin, and the other in Bangor, Maine. He also owned a four-seater Comanche propjet airplane. Seven HMOs operated through the Williams clinic. I managed all emergencies on weekend evenings and night.

In December 1984, Dr. Jasper asked if I would fly with him to Bangor, Maine. His television station was having a Christmas party. We lived around the corner from each other. He picked me up in front of my building and took me to his condominium where I met his wife Margaret, and Teddy, his youngest son, who was also a licensed pilot. Once Teddy got dressed, we went to a small airport in Gary, Indiana. Jasper pulled the plane out of its hanger with a wench. The runway had a dusting of snow, and the sky was gray and dreary. Once we reached an altitude of 10,000 feet, there was blinding sunshine. Fifteen minutes into the flight, one could see downtown South bend, Indiana. I reflected on the cartoon series "Jonny Quest," however, he was on a magic carpet floating over pyramids in the desert. I thought about the statistical chance of riding in a private plane owned and piloted by a Black colleague and his son.

When we reached the airspace over Bangor, there was a heavy snowstorm with little visibility. But Jasper and Teddy performed an instrument landing. We touched down softly on the foot of snow. There was a strategic air command base next to the runway – You could see the B52s parked in their huge garage hangers. Our plane slid to the dock of the Hilton Hotel. We were the only Black people present at that event. I sat next to Dr. Jasper at a large oval boardroom table. He introduced me to a lot of people who operated his Channel 7 affiliated television station. After a few minutes, I excused myself and sat with Teddy at another table. They brought us lobster, king crab legs, and champagne to wash it down. Early the next morning, Jasper was up calling weather stations. He told me how blacks operated in the corporate world. On the way back, we landed in Mansfield, Massachusetts. That is where I met Marie Brown, Teddy's future fiancée. She attended a private school there. They spent some time together, and then we flew back home.

On Sunday April 16, 1985, Diane, my wife, brought dinner to the clinic about 10:00 p.m. She spent time with me until after 2 a.m. I usually answered the phone in Dr. Jasper's big corner office, surrounded by his degrees, awards and photos of him with three Republican U. S. Presidents. The Williams family of Chicago is one of the most influential Black families in the country. At approximately 2 a.m., a disheveled man with a foul body odor entered the waiting room. The guard voiced his displeasure with the man's foul body odor and asked him to leave the waiting room area. He sprayed air freshener to dampen the odor, but at one point he overdid it. Diane freaked me out when she said, "At first, we were smelling the air freshener. Now, what we are smelling is the fragrance of freshly cut roses. Don't you know what that means?" I looked at her with amazement and said, "No." "It is an old saying that if you smell fresh cut roses, someone close to you has died!" she said. I told her to go home because she was spooking me out. She left the clinic just after 3 a.m.

At that time, I was a second-year resident at the Illinois State Psychiatric Institute (ISPI). On the Monday morning of April 17, 1985. I picked up breakfast at a White Hen Pantry close to my office at ISPI. Along with a meal, I usually picked up a copy of Chicago's big three newspapers: Chicago Sun Times, The Tribune, and Chicago Defender Newspapers. I laid the papers on the desk in my office and ate breakfast. About 9:00am, Karen Evans called. She asked if I had a copy of the Defender Newspaper, and then hung up. I reached for the paper and saw the Headline, "Prominent Doctor Killed in Plane Crash!" I could not believe what I was reading. The other two major Chicago newspapers ran the story on page 2. There were old photos of Dr. Jasper and his wife in their young days sitting on the wing of his plane. The articles stated that Dr. Jasper flew the plane to Jamaica with his wife Margaret, his son Teddy, and his fiancée Marie. Their trip was a weeklong engagement vacation. On the return trip home, Dr. Jasper landed in Miami so that Margaret could take a commercial plane back to Chicago. (I knew from experience that the four-seater did not have a restroom.) Dr. Jasper landed at a small airport in Terre Haute, Indiana. He was low on fuel. Shortly after takeoff, the article said the plane radioed an engine problem and crashed into a cornfield one mile from the airport.

I rescheduled all my patients that day. I remembered what Diane said the night before. When she walked through the front door, I thought that she was going to remind me of the previous night. But she was calm and sensed my psychic pain. Diane started calling her political connections. When she got off the phone, she asked me to go with her to the A.A. Raynor and Sons Funeral Home on East 71st street. Mr. A.A. (Sammy) Raynor Jr. escorted us into his office. (The Raynor funeral home received national attention when they hosted the wake and funeral for Emmitt Till in the 1950s.), Sammy Raynor Jr. was a legend in his own rite: himself: a highly decorated WWII United States Air force bomber pilot; an original member of the Tuskegee Airmen. He was a former sixth ward Chicago alderman, and an investigator on the National Transportation Safety Board.

Sammy and Dr. Jasper were close friends, pilots, NTSB investigators, and wealthy Republicans. Sammy had recently returned with the three bodies recovered from the crash site in Indiana. He was part of the NTSB team that investigated the Jasper plane crash. Diane wanted to see their bodies, but Sammy said that Marie Brown's body was the only one not disintegrated in the crash. He had sealed the coffins of Dr. Jasper and Teddy. He said when the plane crashed, there was no fireball, which normally occurs when the wings are loaded with fuel on takeoff. I was confused because he landed there because his plane was low on fuel. Dr. Jasper was a careful man. I won't discuss my thoughts about the matter.

They held Dr. Jasper and Teddy's funeral in the Rockefeller Chapel at the University of Chicago. Diane and I sat in a section reserved for employees of the Williams Clinic. Dr. Jasper's obituary was an ornately decorated book. He crammed lots of living into his sixty-seven years on this Earth. They held a repast in the basement of the Seaway National Bank.

Diane had talent but sabotaged our marriage by trying to rapidly change every aspect of my life. I had no problem with a purely political marriage. She never cooked or kept my place clean. Dealing with her involved too much of what I did not have, patience! We tried to make things work, but I ended up letting her have my lakefront apartment and moved back to Oak Park. The divorce cost a lot of money, but we got along much better as friends.

You learn a lot about yourself when living with another person. As a second-year resident in the medical specialty called psychiatry, I had yet to develop the skilled observation towards human character. Diane had never been married or lived with a man. She thought that I was going to shower her with perpetual attention and affection. She was a physical fitness buff who ran two miles along the lakefront every morning, lifted weights, and went roller skating every weekend. However, she did not cook a meal or clean up at any time during our brief marriage. Both of us were accustomed to living the single life. What alienated me the most was her controlling and possessive tendencies. She never told me about her history as a police officer prior to our marriage. One day, I found a shirt with the Chicago police logo on the shoulder. That is when she came clean about her past. It explained a lot of her behavior. I could not give her what she seemed to want from a man. I was not going to accept having my pants and wallet searched every day when I arrived home from work. The court granted me a divorce from Diane after a year of marriage. But I aged many years going through that stressful process.

In April 1988, I was about to complete my psychiatry residency in a few months; and accepted the position of medical director at Cumberland Hall in Hopkinsville, Kentucky. Before leaving Chicago, I visited JPH to say goodbye to the staff. It was noon when I entered the back entrance of the Family Practice clinic. There was Tracy Pierson sitting at the reception desk. She noticed me walking down the long hallway and met me halfway. Tracy had developed into a perfect 5ft 10in beauty, in every aspect. She walked up and put her arms around my neck as our lips met. She whispered, "I've been in love with you for a long time." She locked the clinic door, held my hand, and led me into an examination room where she turned the lights off.

Things had started much differently between us. I met Tracie Pierson as an intern at JPH. She was in her late teens, tall, and attractive with a bright smile. Whenever I saw patients at the Family Practice clinic, she found a way to get my attention. One afternoon, Dr. Costanzo, the clinic director, saw us lollygagging at the front desk and summoned me to a back office and said "Dr. Johnson, Tracie has a crush on you. But she is only seventeen years old." I reassured him there was nothing going on between us. At the time, Sparkle, my fine-ass girlfriend came to the clinic on Fridays to pick me up. Tracie saw her many times, but it didn't stop her flirtations. I completed the family practice internship at J. P. H. and entered a psychiatry residency at the Illinois State Psychiatric Institute. It was many years before I saw Tracie again.

Tracie lived at home with her mother on the far south side of Chicago. Her mother was a post office supervisor at the downtown branch. Porsche, her younger sister, was in the Navy and married to another sailor. Her father was a Chicago Police Detective who also owned a fugitive apprehension agency. He was known as "007." Detective Pierson was a star linebacker in college and a popular jazz singer at a club called the "Other Place," a popular southside jazz club.

I spent time together with Tracie and her mom. We would all sit back, watch TV, and munch on buttered popcorn. Tracie and Porsche grew up with a lot of attention and support from their parents. Tracie had a brand-new car in the garage that she had never driven.

I will never forget the time when she went with me to my aunt's home after her son was killed. In early May 1988, Kenneth, my aunt Gwen's son, was stabbed in the head with an ice pick by his brother-in-law on the El platform at 35th and Dan Ryan. I had only seen him a few times at family events. Watching my aunt Gwen cry brought me to tears. Tracie knew the art of being supportive.

I was working long hours over the weekends at the Pontiac state prison. The trip was brutal. Tracie called and asked me to come by the "Other Place" when I got home. She said her father was performing that night. That Saturday night, I entered the nightclub's side door. I looked around the crowded dance floor and saw Tracie making her way through the crowd toward me. She was wearing a slick cocktail dress and led me to a banquet table with a vase of flowers in the center. Already seated at that table was my half-brother Kirk, a vice-president at Amazon, and his wife Toni; Liz, my half-sister, she was director of operations and membership for the National Association of Black MBAs; and Mr. James Crooks (CB), my great uncle, who was a wealthy realter that sat on the Chicago police oversight committee. (His son Archie was a police commander in the Grand Crossing district.) CB and detective Pierson were close friends and fraternity brothers.

The four members of my family sat facing Tracie, her mother, and me. I have no idea how Tracie pulled this off. There is no way I could have summoned my relatives to an event like this.

Detective Pierson was a well-built six-foot-four inches tall man. He sang four songs before an intermission. Then he made the announcement. "I want to announce that Tracie, my oldest daughter, is engaged to marry Dr. Van Johnson." We stood up to the rousing ovation. Her father came to our table and sat next to my uncle CB. They had a lengthy private conversation. Tracie's mother was silent the entire evening. I sensed that she did not want to let go of her daughter.

When Ada Phillips, the social columnist for the Chicago Defender Newspaper, noted my appointment as medical director in her social column, CB decided to give me a going away party at his "Pill Hill home." A live jazz band performed at the event. My sister Liz brought a cake with the icing image of a black doctor wearing a lab coat with a stethoscope around his neck. There were many well-known politicians, family, and frat brothers that attended my party. Ada Phillips stopped by and took photos, which appeared in her social column. Tracie came with her mother. It was a memorable occasion. Everybody had an enjoyable time at my celebration.

My days in the 'City of Big Shoulders' were winding down. Tracie's mother invited me over for dinner. But when I arrived, Tracie was not at home. This gave her an opportunity to inform me about Tracie's medical history and allergies. It was too much information for me. She talked about her daughter as if she was still a child. Then came a strange statement from her that I could never forget. "Van, if you knew what I know about my daughter, you wouldn't marry her!" I should've but did not ask her, "Why?" I remained silent. Why would she screw up her own daughter's future with that type of poison? When Tracie arrived home, we continued as usual. I never mentioned what her mother told me until she moved to Kentucky.

When I was a first-year resident at ISPI, I rotated through various departments at Cook County hospital. That is where I had the opportunity to meet and work with sharp black doctors like Dr. Linda O'Bannon, Dr. Waverly Clanton, III, and Dr. Tony Harmon. Dr. Harmon lived two blocks from me on Lakeshore drive. We spent time together on the 55th street beach at "The Point" In Hyde Park. He was a "Lady's Man" who attended Brown University College and Medical School. Tony did not have a chip on his shoulder like most black doctors I met during training.

During the second and third years of training at ISPI, we had numerous exams. On Thursdays, we had to run a morning and afternoon management clinic, which meant monitoring the medications of patients recently discharged from the inpatient units. A team of psychoanalysts and psychologists were responsible for our training. Psychiatry specialists trained us in family therapy and consultation/liaison psychiatry. It was a rigorous training program, but we had less call nights, and more free time than residents in family practice, internal medicine, or surgery training programs. We were only on call once every two weeks in the second year; no call nights for third and fourth-year residents.

I spent most of my free time moonlighting as a staff psychiatrist at the Lawndale and Englewood city-run mental health clinics; the Bobby E. Wright Comprehensive mental health center; Pontiac and Joliet prisons in downstate Illinois. I presented seminars on psychiatric disorders in the elderly at the Niles Township Sheltered Workshop.

Dr. Nathaniel Taylor Winston was president of the Cumberland corporation that owned Cumberland Hall. During my interview with Dr. Winston, he persuaded me to come there for the experience. He built several hospitals and was a southern aristocrat: two great-uncles were governors of Tennessee; one cousin was governor of Georgia; great-grandfather a Confederate army general; grandfather a valedictorian at the Virginia Military Institute. In 1925, his father owned the largest number of Savings and Thrift companies in the state of Tennessee. Dr. Nat Winston was a psychiatrist and former commissioner for the Tennessee Department of Human Services. He was a member of the Grand Ole Opry and won a Grammy for a music book.

It was my first experience living in the rural south. I learned that white supremacy is the governing philosophy everywhere in this country. Prior to my arrival, the corporate headquarters secretly stripped away most of the authority and power from the position of medical director at Cumberland Hall. They did not want me to have the sole power to hire or fire anyone! I could not hire or fire anyone without first going through an executive committee – In essence, I had a position stripped of its power!

I leased a mansion in an exclusive all-white subdivision called Great Oaks. In August, Tracie moved in with me. She had no problems with hospital staff hanging out at my home on Thursdays after work. She complained about it being too quiet at night. Having been raised on Chicago's southside, she was used to hearing sporadic sounds of gunfire and the sirens of emergency vehicles. Tracie had no skill in the kitchen. She did not even know how to prepare bacon and eggs. Thank God, I had a housekeeper. She wanted to have four children. I asked, "How will you care for them?" She responded, "My mother will help out." She was still being treated as a child by her mom.

Tracie had relatives in the Hopkinsville area. We started visiting them quite often. The matriarch of that family was in her eighties. Latham and Donald, her two sons, lived with her. Latham was employed at the Cayce light store on Ft. Campbell Blvd. in downtown Hopkinsville. He was a member of the Pioneers Club, a black social club in the area. Donald was a hunter and took care of their home. On one occasion, Donald was excited after hunting a large Groundhog. The carcass resembled a giant Rat, or Beaver. He invited us to dinner, saying it would taste good in a stew. However, we found a host of excuses to miss that event. Tracie got angry at me for calling them black Beverly Hillbillies.

At the hospital Christmas party, Dr. Sid Levy, the executive director, danced with Tracie several times. I noticed him checking her like everyone else there.

We attended the Pioneer's Club Christmas party. All the elite black folks in the county were at this event. We met the county's first Black sheriff, and other so-called elite black folks in that area.

The warning Tracie's mother gave me ate at my mind like cancer. I finally told Tracie. She had no response. I should have asked her mother for clarification on that matter.

After moving to Kentucky, I became a member of The Association of the United States Army. Tracie and I started going horseback riding at the Fort Campbell army base. It was a twenty-minute drive from my home. It was a place to go when we got bored.

The Jenny Stuart Hospital was across the street from Cumberland Hall. They promised to send me an application to join their staff, but never did. Dr. Winston had a speaking engagement there one evening and took me along. The medical staff marched in and filled the auditorium. It was strange to see only white males. There was not one woman, nor any foreign doctors. Now, I understand why they never sent me an application. A white nurse at Cumberland Hall told me a horrific story about Jenny Stuart Hospital. "They ran a Black surgeon out of town before you arrived. Whenever the black surgeon was on call, they secretly referred patients with private insurance to the white surgeons, which left him with the lower paying patients with Medicare or Medicaid. His wife was a nurse. The all-white nursing staff harassed her every day. They did not think that she should be working as a nurse. Since she did not need it because her husband was a surgeon, she was taking a job from some white nurse."

A recruiter from Las Vegas contacted me about a private practice opportunity in Anderson, Indiana. I initially dismissed the idea, but then realized that my mentors and colleagues all had private practices. I gave the recruiter permission to be contacted by a representative from St. John's Hospital of Anderson.

I was contacted by Dr. Eugene Roach, a psychiatrist on St. John's Board of Directors.

In January 1989, I went to my first interview at St. John's hospital in Anderson, Indiana. I was interviewed by Dr. Eugene Roach, Mr. James Moore, vice-president of hospital affairs, and Mr. James Stephens, president of St. John's medical center. They focused the discussions on my hobbies and lifestyle. I was frank with them. No, I do not play golf. Dr. Roach took me on a tour of the Anderson Center, a private psychiatric facility owned by the hospital. It was located across the street from St. John's hospital. Then we went on a tour of the medical center. The campus was large with a lot of modern buildings.

The next day, Dr. Roach took me on a tour of the city. He said General Motors operated seventeen factories that ran three shifts, seven days a week, and employed thousands of workers. St. John's hospital supplied their medical needs. He stopped in front of the parking lot for several factories and said, "Look at all those cars. Each represents the potential of getting some of that premium GM insurance money."

I had a total of four interviews over a five-month period. At the last interview, Dr. Roach made me a proposal. "St. John's would guarantee an annual income of $120,000 a year through a 'draw', provide a furnished office with a manager in their professional building, and cover my malpractice insurance. I asked if the "draw" was a loan. Dr. Roach replied, "It is not a loan. However, you must admit your patients to our hospital. Those admissions cover the cost of your recruitment."

I discussed everything about that practice opportunity with Tracie. She didn't like it and wanted us to move into her mother's home back in Chicago. I had a lot of trepidation about that idea. Tracie asked to go with me to Indiana. Then she remarked, "I have a feeling that if you go there something bad is going to happen." I loved Tracie and had to protect her safety. The last thing I wanted to do is place her in harm's way. It was no secret that Indiana had a lot of white supremacist groups. I knew that things could get rough and tumble in that white world.

However, Tracie continued to badger me every day about starting a family. She wanted a baby to keep up with her younger sister Porsche, who was married to another sailor and now pregnant. Tracie dreamt of her and Porsche's children growing up together—at least being near the same age. Her obsession with childbirth overshadowed everything that I wanted to accomplish. She never attended college or had an apartment of her own. My goal was career stabilization before starting a family. Simultaneously, I was obsessed with some deeper issues about having children: America's racially toxic culture places Black children in peril from birth. I was frightened by the prospect of being a father. Regrettably, I maladaptively resolved our different agendas by putting Tracie on a bus back to her mother's home in Chicago. In retrospect, I should have gone back to Chicago with her, but then?

In May 1989, I agreed and became the first black psychiatrist in history to start a practice in Anderson, the seat of Madison County. However, the contract I received was ambiguous and lacked clarity on specifics already discussed during the interviews. I contacted Dr. Roach, brought up the inconsistencies, and canceled everything. Dr. Roach called me every night apologizing with assurances that the contract would be corrected by the time I arrived. Mr. James Moore, the vice president of hospital affairs, asked me to choose a moving company to transport my property to Anderson. When I told him about the Mayflower moving company, he replied, "Wheaton moving company will be transporting your property." I didn't have a choice in the matter.

During my last interview in Anderson, I leased an apartment at Crosslake Apartments, a luxury housing complex adjacent to a lake and golf course. Anderson was thirty miles north of Indianapolis. In 1989, it had a population of 60,000. General Motors operated seventeen plants that operated twenty-four hours, seven days a week. Black people migrated to Anderson for employment at the factories during WWII. They were given the dirtiest jobs, but it was wartime and the equipment had to be manufactured for the Army. Black people formed a small community on the west side of town. The white doctors at St. John's and Community hospitals did not treat black patients prior to the 1964 civil rights bill. Black patients traveled to Indianapolis for medical treatment.

When I arrived in town, I went directly to Mr. James Stephens's office. Dr. Roach was already there waiting. He routed me into another office and then handed me two $298,000 one-year term life insurance policies. They were underwritten by John Hancock and contained riders for double indemnity in case I died of accidental death within a year. The St. John's hospital corporation was the beneficiary of one policy, and my parents the other. Dr. Roach assured me that every physician they recruited had to sign insurance policies to cover the hospital's investment. When I asked why he did not inform me of this during the four interviews, he did not answer the question. I asked if signing them was mandatory. Mr. Stevens appeared out of nowhere and said, "Yes." They knew that if I were told about this during an interview, I would not have come to Anderson. In the field of medicine, it is called informed consent: Before any medical procedure, we must explain the benefits and possible complications of any particular procedure. What they did was recruitment fraud!

Wheaton moving company did not transport my belongings to my apartment until two long weeks later. This was the leverage they used to back me into a corner. They were showing me their power! When I signed the two insurance policies, Dr. Roach handed me a revised version of our contract. Ironically, there was fine print on the bottom of the last page: The so-called "draw" was now a $150,000 loan at a 3% interest rate. I told Dr. Roach that they had committed straight-up recruitment fraud. "What person would borrow $150,000 at 3% interest to open a medical practice in this one-horse town?'" He turned red when I asked for the loan check instead of starting a practice. If I were a violent man, Mr. Stephens and Dr Roach would have been executed that morning!

When I walked out of the office with Roach and Stephens, Mr. James Moore was standing in the hallway. He asked me to follow him to his office. Once inside he said, "I am sorry to inform you that we don't have any available office space in the professional building. What are you going to do now?" Moore said that he would ask a black internist if I could share her office, and then mentioned that his wife was on the board of Wheaton moving company.

These hospital officials lured me to this town under false pretenses, and then breached their contract by not having an office space for me to start a practice. I had the intuition that the large insurance policy created a moral hazard and put me in danger of assassination. Bored, wealthy, white men do this type of shit for fun-and-games.

A week after signing the bogus contract and insurance policies, the Wheaton moving company finally brought my belongings to the apartment. What would have happened if I didn't sign the insurance policies? Mr. Stevens would have told me to find a practice elsewhere and not paid Wheaton's bill for moving my property. In response, the moving company would have held my property in storage until the bill was paid and the management at Crosslake Apartments would have voided the lease. They had lured and trapped me in a dangerous situation. I had no option but to play the game until another opportunity became available to me.

I was the only Black person living at Crosslake Apartments. It really was not a luxury complex because there was no security. They did not believe it was needed because the surrounding community was all-white, as well. I was given an apartment in the most isolated section of the complex. There were no lamp posts to light up the area around my place at night. It was a two-bedroom apartment; each bedroom had its own washroom, and window facing the lake. The living room had a genuine wood burning fireplace. The only red flag, there was only one door to enter and exit! My living room did not have a ceiling light fixture.

Dr. Beverly Perkins Edwards was a black internist who had cancer and worked part-time. She allowed me to share her office on a part time basis—eighteen hours a week, which is less than part-time. The St. John hospital officials used her as their intermediary to communicate with me.

After interviewing many candidates, I decided to hire a middle-age white woman named Jackie Hill to be the office manager. She was married to Ron, a supervisor in one of the local factories. They had two teenage daughters. Jackie had managed four psychiatric practices.

Dr. Edward's office was too small to accommodate the patients from both practices. I hated seeing Jackie having to sit on the floor to do her job. Sometimes, I could not evaluate new patients because of the crowded conditions in Dr. Perkins' small office. There was one examination room, but no offices. Jackie once opined, "Those hospital officials are setting you up to fail, which I think is racially motivated."

I could not find any native blacks of Anderson to be my housekeeper(s). When I mentioned the Crosslake Apartment complex in interviews, they recoiled in fear. One young black lady told me, "Dr. Johnson, if you had grown up in this town, you'd know that white folks would attack you in the area where you live. Black people just do not go on that side of town!" I was left with no other option but to hire two young white women who Jackie had recommended. They were in their mid-twenties; both were married and only cleaned the homes of doctors and lawyers in Anderson.

I knew that Dr. Edwards was monitoring me for her white masters. She often tried to impress me with bizarre or elaborate-sounding psychiatric diagnoses. Jackie thought she was crazy. I felt she had suffered from some type of mental breakdown in the past. (I met a psychologist who practiced with the Mid-America consultants in Indianapolis. When I mentioned Dr. Edwards, he responded, "She had been admitted to the inpatient psychiatric unit on numerous occasions throughout her medical career.")

Mr. Stephens and Dr. Roach never introduced me to the chair of psychiatry at the hospital. I was never placed on their psychiatry night call schedule. They brought me there to build an inpatient practice, yet they were impeding my efforts to build that practice through their emergency room.

During my four interviews, Dr. Roach never mentioned the presence of a Black community in Anderson. I saw Black housekeeping workers in the hospital and became curious about their domicile. Since I was restricted to a less than part-time operation, it left me with time to explore the town. I joined the Excel health club near my apartment complex and befriended some black engineers that worked at General Motors. They told me about the 'EL Morocco,' a black owned tavern with the rowdiest reputation. It was the first place I went to mingle with the natives; and soon began visiting the other four black-owned bars to pass out business cards and meet the masses.

Anderson College is the seat of the national headquarters for the Church of God. The town closes down on Sundays, which is when the bootleggers make their money. Saint Mary's catholic church administrated St. John's hospital and was the third largest employer in the county.

I always had a feeling that my actions were being monitored. Patrons at the clubs often offered me free drinks, but I refused. I knew that a D.U.I. would land me on the front page of the *Anderson Herald Bulletin*, the only newspaper in town. One day, Jackie confirmed my suspicion through a snide remark, "There's a rumor that you like the low-end women." I told Jackie that black women lacked only the money and access to the education that white women have.

Each Sunday, I attended a different black church in Anderson. The pastors of the Allen A.M.E., the Baptist and COGIC denominations shook my hand, but never introduced me to their congregations. The Black church leaders may have viewed me as a potential competitor. In medicine, of all the primary care specialties, psychiatry is the least understood and revered in the black community. It has a long brutal history when it comes to blacks(slaves): During slavery, the psychiatric community listed slaves that ran away from captivity as having, "Drapetomania", a psychotic disorder; Willie Lynch, a psychologist, produced instructions to southern plantations owners on how to better control their slaves. Most of the psychiatry icons of the 19th and 20th centuries came from fascist European countries. When I started psychiatry training, there were only 400 black psychiatrists in the entire country.

One afternoon, Dr. Edwards took me by the Sherman Street Church of God to meet Reverend Mel Goode, Jr. He was the pastor. Dr. Edwards was receiving counseling from him about the anxiety secondary to her terminal cancer. (His father, Mel Goode Sr., was the first black national broadcaster in history to anchor network news. Like myself, he was an "Alpha".) One morning, the reverend stopped by my office with an invitation to attend church services on the upcoming Sunday. I arrived for the 11:00 a.m. service and barely got a seat in the packed sanctuary.

DR. VAN JOHNSON, M.D.

When Rev. Goode finally stepped on stage, he looked around the audience until he spotted me. He took the mic and asked me to stand, and then introduced me to the congregation. I received a standing ovation. After the service, many parishioners asked for my business card. Many of them had impressive credentials in various professions and drove to Anderson from Indianapolis. He was the only black pastor to introduce me to his congregation!

One morning, I received a call from a man who identified himself as Dr. Robert Lackey. He requested that we have lunch. We agreed on a date, and to meet in front of St. John's main entrance. I had no idea what specialty he represented and anticipated a successful man behind the wheel of a BMW, Mercedes, or Lexus. On the day of our agreed rendezvous, I started standing in front of the hospital entrance prior to noon. Time slowly went by as no new vehicle stopped in front of the main entrance. At ten past noon, I wondered if he had forgotten. But then noticed an old beat-up, heavily rusted, 1963 black Fleetwood Cadillac sitting on the down ramp. As I got closer, there was a clothes hanger holding the car's taillight to its rear fender. The car had been sitting for at least ten minutes. However, my preconceived notions about his status blinded me to the possibility that he may be driving that "sight for sore eyes," so to speak. When I walked up to the tinted passenger-side window, the driver leaned over and unlocked the passenger door. Once I was in, Dr. Lackey broke out into a gut-wrenching laugh. He wanted to correct any misperception of his success, "I only drive this car to golf outings, and assure you there's two brand new Cadillacs sitting in my garage."

Dr. Lackey was a tall, distinguish looking black professional who was a native of Indianapolis. He graduated from the Indiana University School of Dentistry. For over thirty years, his dentistry practice was in the downtown ABC Bank building. He was the first and only black dentist in Anderson. Anna, his wife, had a Doctorate Degree in Education.

Once we arrived at a country club, Dr. Lackey asked, "Why do you think I invited you to lunch?" I did not have an answer. As I stepped out of the car, Lackey pointed to the rear windshield. I walked to the back of the vehicle and saw the coat of arms for the Alpha Phi Alpha fraternity on a rear windshield decal. He mentioned reading my professional pro-file in St. John's hospital newsletter. I was happy to meet another frat brother. Dr. Lackey knew about everyone at that club. They greeted him with a smile as we were escorted to a corner table overlooking the fairway of the golf course. He took me to the monthly frat meetings in Indianapolis. We often visited each other's homes.

Sonja and I restarted what amounted to our on-and-off relation-ship. We met during my neurology rotation at Cook County Hospital. She was an administrative assistant there and a close friend of Dr. O'Bannon. I also observed her at all the parties held by the black doctors at Cook County hospital. Sonja graduated from the University of Illinois Champaign. Her father was a Jamaican physician who died and left her a duplex in Hyde Park. She was attractive, dressed very well, had her own place, loved to travel, and made a good salary. We often took trips to various parts of the Bahamas and Jamaica. We loved the Caribbean.

We dated, and spent time together, and then went our separate ways, without prejudice. Unlike the other women I dated, she had a lot going for herself and did not need to trap a guy through pregnancy. Both of us were hesitant to bring children into the world. She was her father's only daughter; I was my father's only child until he married many years later. We had talked about a five-year plan to save our money and move to Africa. We visited each other quite often. I didn't mind the three-hour drive to Chicago. Our only quest? To please each other whenever we were together! She had grown up around medical doctors and did not freak out if I went to sleep at a party, after call night.

Jackie and the rest of my staff liked Sonja so much, they would pick her from the airport whenever she flew into town. She'd hang out with Jackie at the front desk.

Chapter Two

AUGUST 1989, MR. JAMES MOORE NOTIFIED ME OF AN abandoned Hollon pharmacy building located in a strip mall across the street from the medical center. While Mr. Moore, Jackie, and me were touring the site, Mr. Moore sarcastically asked if I really wanted to start a practice in that old building. I told him my purpose for coming to that town was to start a practice. Working to build this empty structure was far better than being in a crowded office for a few hours a week. I told Moore that the location was ideal and gave him instructions on the color scheme for each room; and Jackie gave input on her future reception area.

The hospital maintenance department painted the rooms as requested. I spiffed up the office with a sofa, several chairs, end tables, a large area rug, a painting on the wall; I placed trays of candy, peanuts, and magazines on the end tables. Jackie was happy with her large desk. A computer and file cabinets lined the walls of her reception area. The hospital reneged on its promise to install carpeting. I thought it was important with patient privacy. Carpet dampens all types of noise, including sensitive conversations.

At the time, I rarely drank coffee. But I learned something from Jackie, who purchased a large coffee maker that brewed four assorted flavors simultaneously. "White Folks love coffee in the morning," she said.

Once we established a consistent rhythm, I would often drive to the black side of town at lunchtime. My destination was a club named the "Wagon Wheel," a bar and grill owned by a young black business-man. His eighty-seven-year-old mother cooked chitlins year-round. She suffered from polyarthritis. I often brought her samples of the most up-to-date medication for that condition. She taught me a lot of history about the town's legacy of racism and corruption. She usually gave me a plate of chicken wings and French fries.

While I was in the hood taking history lessons during the lunch hour, Jackie's upper-crust girlfriends turned the office into a lunchtime hangout. I thought having wealthy white women spending time together in my office was good for business: It signaled that I was a less threatening negro.

My schedule of new patients was rapidly filling up the time slots. It surprised me that most of them were middle and upper-middle-class whites; skilled tradesmen employed at General Motors. What surprised me the most was the number of patients from the town of Elwood. It is a small, all-white town nine miles north of Anderson; with the reputation of being a "Sundown" town with a largest Klavern in central Indiana. One of my patients claimed to be the daughter of the KKK Grand Cyclops. She never missed a session. She would start by telling me all the Klan activity that took place. I perceived this as a defense mechanism. I asked if her father knew she was seeing a Black psychiatrist. She said yes, "My father said that if a Black man became a doctor in this country, it wasn't given to him." I was surprised by that insight!

I started noticing that a number of my new white patients had left the care of other white psychiatrists in the area. In not understanding this phenomenon, I put the issue before several patients. One client was frank and said that his former white psychiatrist shared confidential information with the Anderson police on him. Another white patient summed up a similar reason. "Dr. Johnson, as a Black man, I know that you aren't welcomed to drink with the other psychiatrist at the country club. I do not have to worry about you revealing my secrets." They changed psychiatrists to safeguard their privacy!

I received a call from the secretary for Judge Thomas Newman, a Madison County circuit judge. She asked if I was interested in evaluating inmates from the county jail. The court needed to know if the inmates were competent to stand trial or not. When I asked about the financial arrangements, she replied, "You determine the price of your services."

On Wednesdays, the inmates were transported early in the morning to my office. Additional staff was hired to type up the evaluations for the court.

Lt. Lee George was an African American sheriff deputy who oversaw the transport of the inmates to my office. After we became acquainted, he was a regular guest at my home. I liked his style. His father had Podiatry practice in Dayton, Ohio. At the time, I received confidential information from him.

I began to see my practice flourish but received a wake-up call from an unexpected place: One evening, I was at the "Cuz" lounge waiting to shoot pool with a black engineer from General Motors. As I sat at the table, a server named Regina Page asked if I wanted a drink. I declined but introduced myself and handed the attractive young lady a business card. While walking away she glanced at my card and suddenly stopped. She came back to me with a bewildered look on her face, "So, you are the black psychiatrist everyone is talking about around town. My girlfriend dates a black Anderson police officer. Did you know they have you under police surveillance?" I just looked at her in disbelief! I wondered, why were white folks so interested in my life? I did not use or sell drugs, drink in public, or sleep with white women.

The Anderson Center called me to evaluate a so-called "aggressive" negro at the facility. It was a private psychiatric hospital owned by the St. John's hospital corporation. It was across the street from their hospital. As I arrived on the unit, four white nurses were at the nurses' station staring at me with their mouths open. They were in a state of shock. I asked the whereabouts of the patient to be evaluated, they ignored me. Then I saw a black woman wearing a housekeeping uniform. I asked her if the fly of my pant was unzipped. She laughed. "No, it is not. They are reacting to you being the first Black psychiatrist anybody around here has ever seen." She escorted me to the patient's room.

The patient was a healthy middle-aged black man. During my interview, he was calm, polite, and sitting on his bed. Not the "aggressive" beast described to me by the white staff. He admitted to feeling depressed and anxious over the welfare of his fourteen-year-old daughter. She had run away from home several weeks ago. His concerns and feelings were appropriate to the circumstance. There were no psychotic symptoms, he was not a danger to himself, the community, or the hospital staff. Their assessments were racist projections. I rarely went into St. John's hospital, and never been to their doctor's lounge or cafeteria. Those white folks did not hide their racism!

In January 1990, I held a birthday party at the Sheraton Hotel in Anderson. Dr. Beverly Perkins-Edwards was allowed to assist me in planning the event. The party was well attended. As the event was winding down, I stood at the door and thanked the guests as they departed. A dark-skinned Indian handed me two wrapped gifts. I had never met him before but thanked him for the presents. He pulled me aside and introduced himself as Dr. Ramaswamy. Then bragged about his practice netting over a million dollars a year. This "Indian Doctor" asked me to close my practice, transfer all of my patients to his clinic, and be his employee for seven hundred dollars a day with paid malpractice insurance. I just stared at him. Then came the bombshell. "The officials at St. John have had no plans of you becoming a success in this town. That is the reason they never placed you on the psychiatry call schedule. They lured you here because I needed the help. I do need your help." I described their method of recruitment fraud and breach of contract. He replied, "You ain't the first doctor. They pulled that on six other doctors, who have lawsuits against the hospital. If you come and work for me, I will clear up this matter." I asked him, "Why don't you pay me for my practice?' What prevents you from firing me shortly after I become your employee?'" When he could not answer those questions, I knew it was some shit in the game!

On Monday morning, Jackie and I talked about the party. I informed her about Dr. Rama's request. She gasped, as her piercing blue eyes locked on mine. "Dr. Rama is under federal investigation for a multi-million-dollar Medicaid/Medicare fraud operation with St. John's hospital. Don't get involved because you'll end up being their scapegoat." I had no doubts about what she is telling me. Jackie came from one of the most affluent white families in that community. Her father was a well-connected general manager for the largest Chrysler dealership in Noblesville, a town thirty miles from Anderson. He spent time together with Judge Phillippe, the most-tenured judge in town. Her brother was head of the computer department at the Anderson Police Department. I will never forget the day Jackie's father gave her a cotton candy red, two-seater sports car for her birthday. After receiving that confidential information from Jackie, I called Dr. Rama and told him I was not interested in giving up my practice.

In February 1990, I applied for admitting privileges at the community hospital, St. John's cross-town rival. Their department chair scheduled a meeting over lunch. However, we did not have anything to eat, just revelations from the chair. He started by saying that there were already too many psychiatrists in town before I arrived. The population could not support all of these practices, and St. John's hospital knew this fact before recruiting me. Then came his most potent venom. "Dr. Johnson, I do not know why St. John's hospital recruited you to open a practice in this town. You are treating a large number of white patients. You were not trained to treat white people. What you are doing is taking food off our table[sic]. I will not grant you hospital privileges at this time." But more ominous was his last statement. "Now, we have to get rid of two psychiatrists to maintain our incomes!" Prior to my arrival, Dr. Rama, the dark-skinned Indian psychiatrist was the only non-white psychiatrist in town. Now, there were the two of us. His message was clear as day.

On a Saturday morning in March, Dr. Eugene Roach called me to complain that I was not admitting enough patients into the hospital. I reminded him of not being on their psychiatry call schedule and couldn't build up my inpatient census through the E.R. Dr. Roach asked if I had a Rolodex. He then suggested that I have my clinic patients involuntarily committed to their inpatient psychiatry unit. "What you should do is create psychiatric petitions that label them a danger to themselves and the community. Once your patients are admitted to the inpatient unit, another psychiatrist will evaluate and release them within twenty-four hours."

I asked Dr. Roach, "What is the purpose of having my patients involuntarily committed to the hospital and released just twenty-fours later?" He did not answer the question. Dr. Roach went even further. "After you prepare those petitions, call the Anderson police, and identify yourself as a psychiatrist. The police will get your patients at their homes and transfer them to the emergency room for hospitalization." At this point, I knew that a bunch of crackpots were running that medical center. I thought Dr. Roach was joking until I asked him if the police would go along with such a crazy scheme he suggested. He replied, "We hire the Anderson police officers for security when they retire from the department. We own that police department in a sense." I told him that his plan was pure madness, and I wouldn't have anything to do with it. Dr. Roach then threatened me with a peer-review evaluation.

On March 20, 1990, Jackie called me from the office at approximately 7:30 am, to report that when she arrived, the back door of the clinic was wide open. I told her to call the Anderson police and make an official report. By the time I arrived, the police had left without making a report or taking any fingerprints. They did not believe a burglary had taken place because the office was not ransacked. The police never contacted me about the matter. They were too disturbed by my professional certificates on the office walls.

Every week, I took my car to be washed at a facility on 3rd Avenue. I owned a blue, luxury edition Bonneville. When I drove there this Friday in late March 1990, I put it in neutral to be pulled through the cleaning cycle. I sat in an area with fresh coffee and plenty of magazines. Then, a man came running toward the waiting area and asked who owned that blue Bonneville. I raised my hand. He summoned me to walk towards the car. He showed me a large piece of visor that came off the left headlight. I said that a road rock did it. He said, "No. They make visors to withstand that type of impact. Someone with a metal tool did that damage!" He said that piece of plastic would have shredded my tires. I wondered who did this dastardly deed?

A week later, I was at home reading the volume of mail I received daily. Just after 6 pm, someone knocked on my door. I asked, "Who is it?" several times. No one answered the question. After several minutes, I thought someone had dropped off a flier and opened the door. There was a tall white man standing so far from the door, his appearance was obscure. He said he was there to collect the newspaper. I jokingly responded, "Isn't that job for children?!" I told him to send me a bill and never come to my home again! He did not say anything. I shut the door and went back to my activities.

In April 1990, Sonja spent a week with me in Anderson. On Tuesday night, we went out for crab legs at a fabulous bar and grill in the suburb of Castleton. We arrived home at 2 a.m. and planned to sleep later than usual. The next morning on Wednesday April 4, Sonja went to take a shower at approximately 10:00am. On way back to the bedroom, she noticed the front door lock being opened from the outside. No one knocked so she presumed that it was a home invasion. Most burglaries occur during the daytime when most residents are at work. She ran into the bedroom and repeatedly slapped me in the face and shook me until I gained consciousness. She screamed, "Van, someone is breaking into this house!" I awakened to a loud boom, as the door crashed into the safety chain. The door was being pushed so hard from the outside; the nails screeched as the wooden support around the doorframe began to crack. I grabbed my Glock handgun from the nightstand next to the bed and stood cover behind the bedroom door. I screamed several times, "Who is it?" No one answered. I walked into the living room, but the front door was ajar with detached segments of the surrounding doorframe. Since no one answered, I presumed the culprits had run away. However, I was surprised when I opened the door to find a tall, husky white man and a short redheaded white woman standing there wearing street clothes. They were later identified as Sherry Granger and Mr. Latham. Both claimed to have no identification. They had no name badges as well. I asked, "Why did you people burst into my home against an engaged safety latch?" They claimed to be there to inspect the foot-long fire extinguisher.

I showed them the damage to the doorframe they caused. After they were allowed into my home, neither gave an apology for their destructive conduct. Once inside my home, I watched them through the door slit of my den. The small fire extinguisher was only a foot-long canister located next to a water heater in the back of the kitchen. I noticed they did not test the damn thing, but just stood there whispering. They were unaware of Sonja's presence in the home. After they left, Sonya was in such a state of anxiety, I was preoccupied with her anxiety and forgot to report the incident to the management. When Sonya regained her composure, she suggested that I find another place to live and practice. I told her that there were plans for transitioning out of that place!

In April 1990, at a psychiatry department meeting, the agenda noted that my application for staff privileges was incomplete. I needed a letter of recommendation from my last employer. These are routine matters that hospitals resolve before spending money to relocate a doctor to their town. Ironically, hospital officials never told me this during the four interviews I had with them. Why would a hospital pay to relocate a doctor to open a practice, without first conducting a complete background check? If a background check revealed anything negative, why did they bring me there?

I contacted Dr. Sid Levy, the executive director of Cumberland Hall. He was my only boss there. Within days, Dr. Levy sent Mr. James Stevens a letter of recommendation on my behalf. Mr. Steven's secretary informed Jackie when the letter was sent. Nevertheless, St. John has had an agenda of their own. The chair of psychiatry and gastroenterology sent me a letter that my staff privileges were terminated at St. John's Hospital. They gave no reason for their action. The reason for the action? None!

A few days later. I received a letter from Mr. James Stevens that stated my contractual agreement with the hospital had been terminated. Again, no reason was noted for their action.

Jackie wondered what was really behind their rash decisions. She said that I did very well for such a brief presence in that community. "You performed better than the four previous psychiatrists whose practices I helped start." She asked her father to arrange a meeting between me and Judge Philippi. Jackie was also at the meeting. The judge stated that he researched my background and suggested that I seek another practice elsewhere. He instructed Jackie to review St. John's contractual agreement with me, note what agreements and provisions they failed to provide, and then highlight those discrepancies in a letter that would only go to Mr. James Stevens. Jackie's research yielded a booklet of contractual infractions committed by St. John hospital officials. I hand delivered a copy of those contractual infractions to Mr. Steven.

A week later, Judge Philippi requested another meeting. This time, he looked tense and worried when he walked into the room. The judge got right to the point. "Dr. Johnson, I cannot take your case because of the injection of 'race' into a corporate matter. This made me feel uncomfortable. You are a good man and I hate to see you in this circumstance." At our first meeting, the subject of race was never mentioned! I would have been naïve to think that a well-respected white judge like Philippi would challenge St. John's Hospital, the county's third largest employer.

Dr. Beverly Perkins-Edwards referred me to Atty. Patrick E. Chavis, III. I called and scheduled an interview. He was a partner with a downtown law firm in Indianapolis. When I entered the foyer of his office, he was seated with a foot upon the desk. Then he farted! I viewed that as disrespect to me. I looked at him with disgust. This is the daily bullshit we put up with each other. After I filled out an application and gave him a copy of my resume, he interviewed me in a private office. He gave me a lengthy background presentation. His grandfather was a white lawyer married to a black woman; his father was an attorney, an Indiana state Senator, and municipal Judge in Indianapolis. His son, Patrick E. Chavis, IV, was in his last year of law school at Indiana University. Chavis briefly talked about being the son of an attorney running around courtrooms watching his father litigate cases. I explained the situation with St. John's hospital and with living in Anderson. Chavis told me the cost of his retainer fee. I wrote him a check and filled out some paperwork.

About a week later, Chavis made a surprise visit to my office. He spent a lot of time questioning Jackie about how I conducted business. She elaborated on every aspect of the operation. When I closed the office that day, Chavis followed me home in his Lexus. I gave him a grand tour of my place. He spent a lot of time loitering through my library. He remarked, "A person's library gives me an indication of what they feed their mind." While he was browsing, I sat down on a sofa in the living room. Chavis walked out of the den with a masonic bible in one hand and the Master Mason's edition of the Bible in the other. He came up to me and gave the master mason password with the appropriate handshake. Our professional relationship had evolved into a personal friendship.

Sonja came to visit me for a week. Atty. Chavis decided to make a trip to my office. I brought him home to meet her. She cooked jerk chicken and other goodies. Chavis enjoyed himself so much that he invited us to join his family at an event to celebrate his son's graduation from law school. The event was going to take place at the "West End," a reception hall near downtown Indianapolis. Atty. Chavis greeted us at the door. We were escorted to a banquet table to meet his beautiful wife—a black queen who exuded class, charm, and grace. Chavis's brother was an obstetrician in North Carolina. He was taller than me. Sonja and Mrs. Chavis hit it off from the start. If you were to observe them interacting, you would get the impression they were longtime friends. I enjoyed watching two beautiful black queens having an enjoyable time. The entire event was exemplary.

Chavis returned to my home several days later. He illustrated the pros and cons of litigating against a large institution like St. John's Medical Center. I told him a lawsuit was not mandatory; retaining him was a defensive move. I took Dr. Beverly Perkins-Edwards seriously when she told me that I was dealing with some dangerous people. But then, Pat asked a strange question. "A Black man killed four white men; what do you think they did to him?"

I replied, "They hung and castrated his ass."

Chavis answered, "No, they committed him to a mental institution for the rest of his life." I did not understand the off-colored nature of his question, or answer.

In late April 1990, Mr. James Stevens sent me a letter about a meeting scheduled in his office at 4 p.m. on Friday, May 5, 1990. I was bewildered by that action because I did not request a meeting with St. John officials. His letter did not note an agenda. This was some type of setup.

Coincidentally, Dr. Beverly Perkins-Edwards invited me to her home for dinner several days before that meeting. This was not unusual; we had many meals together at various venues. Dr. Edwards told me that Mr. James Stevens did not want me to bring a lawyer to that meeting. She warned me, "You are dealing with some dangerous people."

That meeting/dinner confirmed my suspicion that Dr. Edwards was their informant. Otherwise, why would Mr. Stevens send that type of message through her? What were they planning to do at that meeting? Did they think that I would receive a statement like that and show up without a lawyer? I called Chavis and told him about the message for me not to bring a lawyer to the meeting. He did not say anything.

On Friday, May 5, 1990, Chavis arrived at my office fifteen minutes early carrying a large briefcase. He appeared tense and asked if he could smoke in the office. He was the only person I ever allowed to smoke in my office. After a long silence he claimed, "There's not going to be a meeting today." He insisted on riding with me in my car. I parked in the lot across the street from the main hospital building. We went directly to Mr. James Stevens's office. His secretary was standing with a stack of papers in her hands. Chavis placed his briefcase on a chair and started a conversation with the secretary. He asked for directions to the men's room. But every time she gave directions, he appeared not to understand her instructions. She finally walked with him to the men's room. Once they left the office, I was alone in the office. Mr. Stevens suddenly emerged from a side door in his office. Stevens was a 6'5" former basketball player for IU. He walked up to me and said, "Boy, you were told not to bring a lawyer to this meeting. Who is that man?" Before I could answer, Chavis had reentered the office. Mr. Stevens asked Chavis, "Are you a lawyer?" Chavis reached into the briefcase, pulled out a business card, and handed it to Stevens, they stared each other down like two boxers before a prize fight. After Mr. Stevens read the card, he told Chavis, "Dr. Johnson was told not to bring a lawyer to this meeting. There will be no meeting." Atty. Chavis put his hand on my back and routed me out of the office. As we entered the hallway, two hospital security guards were standing there with their guns drawn.

We went to my apartment after leaving the hospital. Chavis said that it was a set-up, and he was happy to be there. I wanted a more in-depth analysis, but Chavis asked, "What do you think they are doing right now?" He answered his own question. "Mr. Stevens is calling Indianapolis to find out who I am. When he finds out the shit will hit the fan."

I asked, "What would have happened if I had gone there alone?" Pat ignored the question and left for home.

I told Jackie what happened in Mr. Steven's office at the so-called meeting. She was not surprised and revealed a deeper level of hospital corruption. "Seven other doctors have lawsuits against St. John's Hospital with claims of false recruitment and breach of contract. Your case is worse than all of them combined since it is racially motivated. Your lawsuit has the best chance of winning in court. Once its filed, those other doctors with pending cases would join your attorney to create a class action lawsuit."

A week after the canceled meeting, Dr. Beverly Perkins-Edwards invited me to breakfast at the Sheraton Inn. I had a feeling that the real purpose was to relay feedback from hospital officials. She said Mr. Stevens was highly pissed-off at me for bringing Chavis to that meeting. "These are extremely dangerous people. They are coming after your medical license," she said. I thanked her for the feedback and related the message to Chavis.

Within days of talking to Dr. Edwards, Chavis called me to request a meeting in a parking lot adjacent to the Interstate 69 highway that runs through Anderson. I wondered what brought about that unusual location for a meeting. We usually meet in his office, my home or office. I asked Mary, an acquaintance, to accompany and direct me to the site he requested. She was a native of that town and knew exactly where to go. When Chavis arrived, he cut right to the chase "Dr. Johnson, are you on drugs? Are you doing anything illegal?" I said no to his questions. He then warned me, "If you're doing anything illegal, please stop!" Chavis asked Mary, "Does he drink when you're out on the town?" She replied, "We do not date. I have never observed him drinking in public." Before jumping back into his car, he warned me that things were about to get crazy soon. Just days later, I experienced some of that "craziness." Someone knocked out the left headlight of my new automobile.

On June 1, 1990, after my typical Friday afternoon sessions with a male ADHD patient, his mother and I usually talked about his progress. However, after this session, the mother, a General Motors employee, said there was some urgent information I needed to know. But first, she wanted to know if I was in Chicago the previous weekend. When I confirmed my presence there, she told me her niece was a dispatcher for the Madison County Sheriff's Department. Her niece told her that on the previous Sunday morning between 2:00 a.m. and 3:00 a.m., a communication came over the sheriff's radio. "Dr. Van Johnson is in Chicago this weekend." During her thirteen years of employment there, she had never heard that type of communication over the sheriff's radio frequency. The mother asked who damaged my car. "As a General Motors employee, I could get you a replacement for about $350 dollars." I thanked her.

Chapter Three

IN APRIL 1990, I MET DR. W. PERRY PH.D., A BLACK psychologist, at a fraternity meeting. He was a partner in the Mid-America Consultants, a group of Black psychologists based in Indianapolis. He said they had been searching for a long time for a black psychiatrist to join the group. After we exchanged contact information, I was told, "You need to get out of Anderson!" He arranged a meeting for me to meet the group's three black psychologists over lunch. Dr. C. Kegler chaired the group. He asked, "Why in the hell did you start medical practice in Anderson? Don't you know that is in the heart of Ku Klux Klan territory?" I told him that I did not know it. I felt embarrassed. Kegler said they were looking for a black psychiatrist to admit their patients into the hospital. After several meetings, they admitted me into the group as their medical director. They provided me with a furnished office and secretary. The group owned a large court way building. The various apartments were converted into offices, exam rooms, and waiting rooms. They wanted their patients admitted to Winona Hospital, which was located on Meridian Street, directly across the street from their offices.

In the last week of May 1990, I conducted my first weekend clinic at the Consultants office building. (I was still running my full-time practice in Anderson.) When I walked through the door, the office was lined with patients. There was not one empty seat. When I completed the last evaluation, the secretary informed me that there was a six-month waiting list of patients. I had hit paydirt. My clients were the black middle class of Indianapolis. I ran into Dr. Kegler before leaving the office. During our brief discussion, he informed me that the Pendleton Reformatory was seeking a psychiatrist to chair their department of psychiatry.

I called the Pendleton Reformatory and spoke with Mr. Duckworth, superintendent of the facility. After hearing that I had practiced at the Joliet and Pontiac correctional facilities in Illinois, he scheduled an interview with me. Dr. McDaniel, chair of the prison's Department of Education, was also present at the interview. Afterwards, we had some delicious fried chicken for lunch in the prison cafeteria. Duckworth was a hard man to read. He was very observant and had the demeanor of an evangelical pastor. Dr. McDaniel was more aggressive with his questions. One took me by surprise. "Have you ever studied the book, *The Criminal Personality*? When I answered, "many times," I noticed the adrenaline rush through his bloodstream. This book is the Bible in prisons around the world. They were written by Dr. Saminow and Dr. Yochelson. There were three volumes, each containing 600-700 pages. If you read these books, you will know just about every aspect of criminal behavior! After the interview, I drove back to Anderson wondering what they thought of me.

Two weeks later, just before closing my Anderson office on a Friday evening, Jackie announced that two visitors had just walked into the office. Moments later, I was surprised to see Warden Duckworth and Dr. McDaniel enter my office. It caught me off-guard. Duckworth did not waste any time. "Dr. Johnson, how much will it cost to get you to chair our department of psychiatry?" We went back-and forth but eventually agreed on a salary of $135,000 per year. I was required to be at the reformatory on Mondays and Tuesdays. However, I would be on call 24/7 for suicide emergencies; the only ones that required me to report to the prison. The warden pulled a contract out of his briefcase. I read and signed it. Jackie made copies. Duckworth explained that the contract had to be signed by everyone in the chain of command. So, by the end of May1990, I joined a group practice with a new office in Indy, and I signed a contract to chair a department of psychiatry. In a sense, April was my "showers," and May was my "flowers!" Happily, my plan of escape from Anderson was orderly and within the law.

On the upcoming weekend of June 8-10th, I had planned a drive to Chicago and spend the weekend with Sonja. Tuesday, June 5, 1990, Vera Dupree called my home from Fisher—a suburb north of Indianapolis. She claimed to be an undercover state police officer assigned to the international airport. When I asked the reason for the call, Vera said it was something that could not be discussed over the phone and wanted permission to visit my home. I granted her permission. She arrived about thirty minutes later wearing blue jeans, gym shoes, and a lightweight dark jacket. When I asked for proof of identity, she pulled out her state police ID, then opened her coat whereby I could observe the firearm and handcuffs.

Vera was about 5' 4" and appeared to weigh about 110lbs. She was not imposing in any way. She did not strike me as being a policewoman. She refused my offer of refreshments. After several minutes of silence, Vera told me that the state police receive a substantial amount of reliable information every day from confidential sources. She said that they had reliable information that a contract hit was placed on my life in that city and county. "They are planning to stage you in a fatal car crash on your drive next weekend to Chicago. The crash would be made to appear as an accident. We do not know the identity of those on the hit team, but it will include off-duty Anderson police officers and Madison County sheriff deputies," she said. When I asked who had placed the hit on me, she responded, "Officials at St. John's hospital."

I then wondered how anyone knew about my upcoming trip. Vera replied, "There is an illegal wiretap on your office phones. We contacted the Seventh Circuit Court of Appeals in Chicago to ask if a judge had granted a T3 warrant to tap your phones. No judge had issued a T3 (Title Three) warrant to tap your phone." She had not checked to see if my home phone was also illegally tapped. The management of the complex had a passkey to my home. I wondered how many times they entered my home in my absence. Hearing that kind of information is incredibly stressful.

According to Vera, the contract on my life necessitated the state police to open an investigation into my background as well. She told me,

"We know you have an Indiana CCW permit and recently purchased a Glock .9 mm handgun at a sports store in town." I requested police protection, but she claimed that was not possible because I was not an elected official. Their only responsibility they had in the matter was to inform me of the threat. She gave me the following suggestions: postpone that upcoming drive to Chicago; stay away from the black nightclubs; search my office garbage cans every night before closing my office; and keep all the lights out in my home at night. I immediately informed Chavis about our meeting. He only asked for Vera's phone number. Chavis gave instructions to call him if anything unusual happened to me.

I spent that evening on the phone with family, friends, and frat brothers, informing them about the impending date with a hitman. Henry Locke, the managing editor of the *Chicago Defender Newspaper* and frat brother, assured me that his staff would be placed on alert about my situation.

When I sat back and thought about the matter, something profound came to mind, "Why did my death have to be made to appear as an accident?" Then I speculated about their motive: That John Hancock one-year term life insurance policy would expire on the first day of July—just several weeks away. The St. John's hospital corporation was the beneficiary if I died within a year. The policy was loaded with various 'Riders' like Double Indemnity; reimbursement for moving me from Kentucky to Indiana; Jackie's yearly salary; Malpractice insurance; office expenses; my guaranteed income. The "Hit" on my life had to be played out to look like an accident! Why? They could have had me gunned down or stabbed to death at any time. But if they murdered me by the gruesome methods, that insurance company would've dispatched investigators to Anderson. They would not have paid out any death benefits in an obvious murder! (Most of the top insurance companies hire investigators who were former FBI and ATF agents.)

That is why they had to stage me in a car crash that appeared to be an accident. As an alternative, they would also have to hire someone with martial arts skill to beat me to death or break my neck—circumstances where a corrupt coroner could easily label my death an accident.

When I told Sonja about the meeting, she sobbed and asked me to get the hell out of Anderson. I told her that the upcoming drive to Chicago would be cancelled. She agreed to help me find an apartment and scheduled a flight to Indianapolis on the Monday morning of June 11, 1990. Her flight would arrive at 7:00 a.m. I'd have to awaken at 5:00 a.m. to make it there on time.

I informed Jackie about my meeting with Vera. She did not say anything because there were a lot of patients to be seen that day. I asked her to contact the FBI and notify Judge Philippe of the impending threat.

Several days later, I was surprised when Vera returned to my home and asked if I had food in the house, or something that needed to be picked up. She bought groceries, picked up my laundry and clothes from the dry cleaners. I asked why she was doing all of this for me. She said, "It may be the last days I see you alive! That 'Hit' on your life is supposed to take place several days from now."

Saturday, June 9, 1990, there was a room full of patients when I arrived at my new office in Indianapolis. Before leaving that day, I set up two different management clinics because of the substantial number of patients recently discharged from the hospital on medications.

After lunch with my psychology partners, I was introduced to Dr. Randy May, chair of Psychiatry at Winona hospital. Dr. May was cordial and assured me that staff privileges would be granted at their next hospital executive meeting.

While I was in Indy seeing new patients, my housekeepers were getting my home straightened up. I would ride with them in their car to pick up Sonja from the airport early Mondy morning.

Sunday, June 10, 1990, was a warm and sunny day. I had a small concrete patio which led to a narrow entrance to my home. The day was beautiful. One could observe the blooming flowers along the lake shore, just yards away from my front door. That day they were holding the final round of the U.S.G.A. golf championship. Television coverage started at noon. At the time, Tiger Woods was the number one-ranked golfer in the world. Some of my fraternity brothers decided to drive all the way from Indy to my place, to enjoy the coverage with me. Those guys brought all sorts of Chinese cuisine, pizzas, and a variety of cold beers. As the tournament was ending, they helped me clean up the place and left around 5:00 p.m. I had to be up early the next morning to catch that ride with my coworkers to the airport.

Around 6:00pm, an unusual drowsiness forced me to fall asleep on the love seat in the living room. This was followed by the most frightening dream in my life. I saw myself sitting on the patio basking in abundant sunlight, observing the various flowers that had sprung up on the shoreline just feet from my patio. Suddenly, a tall lanky, well-built white man seemed to come out of nowhere and walked upon the patio towards me. As he got close, I stood up to face him. He walked upon me without saying a word, and then placed me in some type of headlock, a chokehold. I struggled and to break his grip without success. He tightened the grip to the point where I could not breathe within a few minutes. As I lost consciousness in my dream, I woke up gasping for air. I was diaphoretic with drenching perspiration streaming down my face. The sheet under me was soaking wet! This dream scared me. I had no idea what to make of it. I walked to the window to look outside and see if I was in the real world. After changing the sheet on the loveseat, that knockdown drowsiness hit me again. I immediately entered another nightmare. I was seated in front of a black movie screen. Major newspaper headlines appeared in front of me like a carousel of images. Each headline presented something about a shooting at my home. For example, "Dr. Johnson shoots intruder!" It was surreal! When I woke up this time, I walked into every room in my home to see if something was wrong. This chain of surreal dreams was beyond my level of consciousness. It was "Twilight Zone" stuff.

I decided to change my setting because that love seat was jinxing me. At approximately 8:40 pm, I went into the guest bedroom (den) and sat in my favorite chair. I put on headphones and listened to my favorite album by a rock group called, The Cars. *Tonight, She Comes* was my favorite song on that album. I played that song whenever Sonja was coming to town. The chair I sat in faced the stacked stereo system, which in turn, sat inches in front of the only window in the room. There was a white silk curtain covering the window. From it, you can see the lakefront during the day, and the front door at any time.

I sat in my favorite chair, clad in only boxer shorts, and started listening to the entire side of the album. The music put me to sleep. When I awakened, every song on that side had been played. The needle was riding the album gutter. As my eyes were acclimating to the darkness, I noticed the black silhouette of a person was in front of the entire window. A small 25-watt bulb over the outside of the front door, projected its shadow over the den window. (I followed Vera's warning to keep my lights off at night.) The figure had that athletic 'T' shape. It was the first time I was paralyzed by fear in my life! The first thing that came to mind was the "hit" on my life. It was terror that only a black soul in America could understand. The well-built features of that phantom image brought law enforcement to mind: most cops keep in good physical shape. Furthermore, Vera said that various police forces would be involved.

After regaining some measure of composure, I eased out of the chair, crawled from the den, and ran into the other bedroom to retrieve my shotgun. I eased back into the living room and watched the menacing black shadow dart from window-to-window of my home. He posted up in front of every window for minutes, but never once knocked on the door. There was no attempt to gain entry through the windows.

He finally posted up in front of the den's window. The apartment door was at a ninety-degree angle to the den's window, which was three feet away. I looked through the peephole, but only the left side of his face and body could be seen. When I opened the door, he just silently stood there staring into the window of the den. Bizarrely dressed in a fur-lined blue winter coat, blue jeans and brown high-heeled, snake-skin cowboy boots. He abruptly turned and rushed at me. I dropped to the floor and fired a round upward. I thought the pellets (a No.4 green sleeve shell) had scattered and missed him when he stopped and stood over me. Less than thirty seconds later, he squatted and fell backward. He did not try to break the fall, which caused a laceration to the back of his head. I knew he was in critical condition. His long legs extended into the living room and prevented me from shutting the door. There was no ceiling outlet for a light bulb in the living room. I turned on an arching lamp behind the love seat and pulled the rest of his long body into the living room and assessed his injuries. His legs were placed in a Trendelenburg position, to redirect blood flow from the lower extremities to the core organs in the upper part of the body. His legs were limp as he had expired. (The Indiana State medical examiner estimated that he died within seventeen seconds of being shot.) I was in a state of shock and failed to search him for weapons.

The decedent was a tall, well-built man with almost no body fat. My first impression was that he was in a paramilitary outfit, or a corrupt police officer carrying out a '" black operation" for someone, or entity. His attire was out of season. Who is going to wear a fur-lined winter coat in the middle of June? That coat was worn as a buffer to soften any blows that came from me in combat and hide his identity during exit.

I had a suspicion that St. John official would one day take my life. That is their reason for trapping me into signing that high yield John Hancock insurance policy. They knew I had joined the Mid-American Consultants in Indianapolis; and signed a contract with the Indiana Department of Corrections to chair a department of psychiatry at the Pendleton prison. My future was promising. However, the officials at St. John's hospital were pure sociopaths! Since I didn't play the game, and hired a lawyer, they felt no other option. They owned the police, elected officials, and judges in town. If I was found dead in my home, they would've ruled it an accident and collected nearly a half-million dollars in benefits, which are untaxed payouts! How many negroes are worth half-a-million? If no money was to be gained, they would've let me leave town unimpeded.

I feared police would summarily execute me when they arrived at my home; and immediately turned on all the lights. Why? The police had me under surveillance for months, and already knew me. Now they're responding to me killing their point man. If they came into a dark apartment, I'd be a dead man! The call itself was evidence that I survived. I remembered Chavis telling me to call him if anything unusual happened. So, I did. His wife answered the phone and said he was asleep. I told her it was a dire emergency. Moments later, I heard his voice on the phone. I told him that I had shot someone. He told me to call the police and hung up. I called 911 to report the incident. Two policemen arrived first, and asked if I knew the deceased. Then came the shocker. "Judge Newman issued a Mississippi-Davis warrant for us to take you to the hospital. They want your blood tested for drugs and alcohol." I called them less than five minutes ago. How did they get that warrant so fast? They asked me what happened. I led them into the den and pointed at the stereo system. The turntable was still running with the needle at the end of a record. I explained that the deceased darted from window to window of my home, and then rushed me when I opened the door. One officer said, "That dead man is a friend of mine. I should shoot your ass right now. Go put on some fucking clothes." As I was being led out of my home in hand-cuffs, a group of police entered, and began to search it without a warrant. A crowd had already assembled on my lawn.

At the police station, they placed me in a room for over five hours. It wasn't until 5 am, Monday, June 11, 1990, that police took me to the emergency room at the Community hospital. An attending physician performed a physical exam and said that my fundoscopic exam showed a blurring of the right optic disc—an indication of very high blood pressure with the risk of an impending stroke. He drew eight tubes of blood for testing.

When I was brought back to the police station, Detective Lt. Richwine took me into a room, read me Miranda rights, and asked questions about the shooting. I repeatedly told him to consult with my attorney, Patrick E. Chavis, III, and even gave him Chavis' phone number. I told Richwine about my plans to pick up Sonja at the airport. He allowed me to call her in Chicago. I told her what happened and to cancel the flight. She cried and screamed, "you should've moved away from that town sooner." Finally, she asked if there was anything that could be done to help. I asked her to contact my family, colleagues, and frat brothers.

After I completed the call to Sonja, Det. Richwine, "Fuck that Miranda bullshit, you're going to tell us what took place at your home!" He turned on the tape recorder. I didn't know the decedent but gave a lengthy statement about the shooting at my home that night – along with everything else that I had experienced in Anderson. Afterward, he escorted me into a large conference room. When I entered, there was an all-white group of male detectives already seated. Lt. Richwine walked to the podium and announced that I would be charged with murder.

Anderson police then transported me to the county jail around 7.00 a.m. At 8.00 a.m., I was allowed to receive a phone call in the cell-block from Mr. Henry Locke, the managing editor of the Chicago Defender newspaper. Henry asked if I was injured by the assailant or beaten by police. I said no. Henry asked if I thought the attack was related to our discussion about the contract hit on my life. "Of course, it is," I said.

On Monday, June 11, 1990, the shooting at my home was also the Headline and Lead story in the Chicago Defender Newspaper.

I was placed in the general population at the jail, as opposed to protective custody. This was planned by the law enforcement officials for several reasons: The cellblocks in jails are teaming with snitches; there was no eyewitness to the incident at my home, so hopefully, they'd wish that I gave a contradictory statement to someone—something they could use against me at trial. Their snitches could monitor my phone calls.

Most of the inmates were watching the morning news and waiting for breakfast. I was unaware of how things operated in jails. As a result, I made a laughingstock of myself: I banged on the cellblock window to get the guards attention in the control booth. He asked if there was something I wanted. I asked for a menu to order breakfast. That request brought roaring laughter from the guard and everybody in the cellblock – I'm talking about a gut-wrenching laugh at my expense. The guard informed me that everyone ate the same thing, every day of the week.

Monday, June 11, 1990, the shooting was the lead story on Channel 8, WISH-TV. A news reporter interviewed detective Lt. Richwine, who said, "The late Mr. James Wagner was married with children and worked as an engineer at General Motors. Dr. Van Johnson shot and killed him when he knocked on the door to collect for his children's paper route."'

How did Richwine know what Wagner did at my home? Chavis said that everyone he interviewed in Anderson said that there were no newspaper collections on Sundays. Richwine never mentioned what time the shooting occurred and didn't speculate on a motive. He did say that a search of my home turned up a cache of weapons. I had no idea that one handgun and one shotgun equaled a cache! Richwine made sure not to mention my concealed carry permit. He ended the interview by saying, "The Wagner family obtained a civil injunction that froze all of Dr. Johnson's assets; he's being held on a 72-hour hold until further investigation.

Later that Monday morning, June 11, they announced over the jail's P.A. system that I had an attorney visit. They transported me to the first floor, where the legal conference rooms were located. When I entered, I saw this ugly-ass negro who identified himself as attorney Montague Oliver—the poster boy for burned-out dope fiends! During my first days in town, people warned me to avoid him! He was an "Alpha," but had the reputation for beating up black women and smoking the Rock(cocaine). Now, I was sitting in a room facing him.

Atty. Oliver said, "The police allowed me into your home last night. I told them that I was volunteering my services on your behalf." I responded, "You aren't my lawyer. Why you lie to them?' Patrick E. Chavis III of Indianapolis is my lawyer. Nigger, did you steal any jewelry from my home?" I told Oliver to stay the fuck out of my business and away from me. As Oliver was walking out, Atty. Chavis entered the room. The two lawyers glanced at each other but didn't exchange words. Once Oliver had left the room, Chavis asked me about him. I told him about all the rumors about Oliver. I told Chavis that Anderson police had allowed Oliver into my home after they took me to jail last night. Chavis looked bewildered and stared at the floor shaking his head disapprovingly.

Chavis had a very serious discussion with me that morning. "Dr. Johnson, you are on the front page of every newspaper in this state. You look guilty because you're a black male in America. This will be a high-profile case. They are going to charge you with murder." When I attempted to describe what happened at my home, Chavis countered, "No one believes anything you have to say! That white man you shot is

James Wagner, a father of three—well-known and liked in this town. He works as an engineer at General Motors and coaches a little league baseball team. His wife sells ads for the largest radio station in this region. Their children have a paper route for the Anderson Herald Bulletin, the only newspaper in town." Chavis asked if I wanted him to represent me in this matter. Again, he brought up his background growing up in courtrooms watching his father litigate criminal cases. He claimed to have first built his reputation as a criminal lawyer in murder trials. Then described the civil matter with St. John's Hospital as a patient with a rash, who developed a serious heart problem. He asked, "Which condition needs to be treated first? Dr. Johnson, this situation you're in now is about your life!" I accepted his invitation to represent me. However, when I mentioned cost, Chavis said that during the night, the decedent's family had a lawyer to file a civil suit and some judge froze all of my assets. "They plan to strip you of all assets by a quick civil summary judgment. I've never heard of anything like this in my entire career," he said. I vehemently asked him not to allow Atty. Montague Oliver on the defense team. He seemed preoccupied and said he had to rush back to Indianapolis.

After that meeting with Chavis, I was escorted into the office of Capt. Doris Maxey, the jail commander. She asked, "Where is the ring?"

I said, "What ring? What are you asking?"

She said, "The dead man's wedding ring."

I told her that I didn't know him and took nothing off his body. I asked her, "I'm a doctor. Why would I take a wedding band from a man who attacked me?" She turned red-faced and had me taken back to the cell block.

An hour later, I was escorted into a room with a closed-circuit television set. A magistrate informed me of the seventy-two-hour hold for the investigation of murder, and I would be formally charged in circuit court.

Tuesday, June 12, 1990, I had another attorney visit. This time when I entered the conference room, three attorneys were present: Attorney Pat Chavis, III, Montague Oliver, Jr., and Tom Broderick Jr. The latter two were from Anderson. Chavis explained that they were going to a court hearing to have the freeze on my assets lifted. I would see him in court. Attorney Carl Blevins filed the civil suit against my estate. He was from a prominent family in Anderson, and a close friend of the Wagner family.

At the court hearing, Atty. Blevins moved the court for a summary judgment against my estate. "Van Johnson knowingly and intentionally killed the late Mr. James Wagner." Atty. Tom Broderick countered, "freezing his assets is unconstitutional. It would deprive him of the right to choose counsel of choice against a pending murder charge. Dr. Johnson has the money to retain the legal counsel of choice, and it would deprive him of that constitutional right if the injunction remained." The judge lifted the injunction.

After the hearing, representatives from ABC Bank and Merrill Lynch were waiting for me at the jail. They liquidated my (401K), IRA, and stock portfolio within minutes. The lawyers behaved like a flock of vultures at a fresh carcass, so to speak. Jackie came to the jail that afternoon and told me that all my patients had paid off their outstanding bills—to the tune of $26,000 dollars. She had placed all the wall certificates and degrees in a large box. The police never entered my office. There was a pauper cemetery within fifty yards from my office; and could be seen from my lobby. St. John's hospital owned it. Jackie said they buried James Wagner there, and the Knights of Columbus held a graveside ceremony for him. I found out from her that Wagner, Mr. Stevens, Dr. Roach and Broderick (my attorney) all attended St. Mary's parish. What an ear full!

After my assets were liquidated, I told Chavis to form a team, but exclude Oliver from it. Despite my objections, he retained Broderick and Oliver. His reasoning for retaining Broderick, "We need a reputable white man like Atty. Broderick, with his background as a prosecutor. It could help me understand the prosecutors' tactics." (At that time, Broderick's father was the Madison County Assessor; his family owned the Broderick Realty Company. They were one of the wealthiest families in that region.)

Chavis then explained why he retained Atty. Oliver. "The police allowed Oliver into your home on the night of the shooting for a reason.

We don't know why. 'What did he do, or witness in your home that night?' If he's on the defense team, they can't use him against you at trial. I will limit his role to just fiduciary matters.'" (I had a hunch that both Chavis and Oliver would one day sell my out, or eventually sabotage my defense.)

The following day, they placed me in the jail's drunk tank, a small white room with a large window and steel bench. It was located directly across the hall from a guard station.

Wednesday, June 13, 1990, a well-dressed, distinguished looking white man entered the drunk tank holding a folder. He sat next to me and whispered, "I'm Dr. Edward Strain, a psychologist from Indianapolis. I'm working with attorney Pat Chavis." He surreptitiously slid me some type of form and a pencil. Dr. Strain instructed me to complete the form on the bench to prevent the guard in the booth from observing what was taking place. Dr. Strain took the completed form and left the room. Minutes later, Chavis entered the room. "You are in big trouble. Those white folks are not playing." He quoted a phrase from his grandfather, "All white folks have pink-asses, and always unite along racial lines." Chavis vehemently warned me not to discuss my case with other inmates, or disclose what took place today with Dr. Strain, and to always remain cool.

Later that afternoon, Atty. Broderick paid a visit and informed me they had hired a private investigator named Richard Martz. His office was in the town of Elwood. Atty. Broderick revealed that police had obtained a warrant to search my home for the decedent's missing wedding band. The wife claimed he was wearing it when he left home. Maybe she needed that cover to conceal what they did in my home. The first thing that came to my mind was that Mr. Wagner had a secret life! I mentioned being questioned about the ring by the jail commander. I asked him, "Why would someone for no reason shoot a total stranger and take their wedding band?"

Before the results of any comprehensive investigation into the shooting, the Wagner family with various police authorities in Indiana used their media connections to initiate a campaign of character assassination against me. Since I was held in custody without a bond, their lies would go unrebutted. It started on the night of the shooting. My aunt, Gloria Davidson, a Cook County sheriff's deputy, called the Anderson police station to check on my whereabouts and general condition. The officer told her, "James Wagner called Dr. Johnson fifteen minutes prior to going over to his home. He wanted to discuss the affair Dr. Johnson was having with his wife. When he knocked on the door, Dr. Johnson shot and killed him." My aunt believed that lie because it came from another policeman. She never tried to contact me to find out the truth. Her jealousy of Barbara, her sister, may have been the unconscious motivation for disseminating that unverified story to the entire family. That lie led to the foreclosure of any support from my family. One cousin summed up the family's collective sentiment, "How can we support a black doctor who killed a white man, over an affair with his wife?"

The investigators told Dr. Albert Rubenstone and Dr. William Thomas at Mt. Sinai Hospital in Chicago, "James Wagner and his son went to Dr. Johnson's home to collect a newspaper bill. An argument ensued and Dr. Johnson retrieved a shotgun. He chased them while firing five rounds. Wagner got tired from running with his son in tow and laid over his son's body. Dr. Johnson ran up and shot the man in the back." When the investigators left, Dr. Rubenstone said, "They're lying on Dr. Johnson!"

The investigators told colleagues at Rush Medical College and the Illinois State Psychiatric Institute, "Mr. Wagner went to Dr. Johnson's home to collect a newspaper debt. Dr. Johnson shot the man through[sic] the door when he knocked." Anderson detectives told Dr. Nat Winston, president of the Cumberland corporation, "Wagner brought his son to Dr. Johnson's home to collect a newspaper debt. There was an argument over the bill. Dr. Johnson told him to wait a minute and returned with a pistol. He shot Wagner in the face as his young son watched in horror. The family couldn't give their loved one an open casket funeral."

Years later, I had a chance to speak with Dr. Winston. After telling him what led up to the shooting at my home, he asked for all the news articles, and anything else related to the case. I sent him a thick folder.

Dr. Winston called several weeks later and said, "I didn't believe their (police investigators) story in the first place. That's why the state of Tennessee never took any action against your medical license. I know everyone on that medical board. You had a lot of money and lived in a mansion. The hospital staff here was shocked when you gave that math teacher a Volvo prior to moving away. I couldn't imagine you shooting someone over a few dollars. The story just didn't sound right.

Dr. Winston ended the conversation, "Dr. Johnson, white folks have been lying about black people for a long, long time."

Those horrendous lies were disseminated within weeks of my arrest. No definitive investigation had taken place. They succeeded in alienating any support from my family and the powerful medical establishment.

Chapter Four

THURSDAY, JUNE 15, 1990, WAS MY FOURTH DAY IN JAIL. I was transferred to a single-man cell with a great view of City Hall. After breakfast and routine jail checks, we were allowed to have outdoor recreation on the rooftop of the jail. It had a basketball court and a panoramic view of the city. A deputy was stationed at the door. When the recreation period ended, I asked him if he knew when I would be able to bond out of jail. The deputy sarcastically replied, "At this very moment, they are having the funeral of that man you shot. If you made bond, you wouldn't make it two blocks."

A guard was waiting for me when I reached the cell block. After being escorted to a holding tank on the main floor of the jail, they placed me in handcuffs and leg shackles. A small group of inmates were also waiting to be transported. Deputies loaded us into several vans and transported us to the county courthouse. The van I was in entered the building through a basement entrance. The defense team was waiting near the bank of elevators. A deputy commandeered an elevator that took us to the second floor. When the doors opened, a crowd of news reporters began taking pictures as their flash bulbs flickered. The lawyers didn't answer any questions. A large crowd of angry-looking white folks was waiting to clear the metal detectors.

Once inside the courtroom, I sat alone. Bill Lawler, the prosecutor, huddled with his chief deputy and my defense team. Judge Fred Spencer, the presiding judge, brought the court to session. Lawler read the indictment against me, "The state of Indiana is charging Van Johnson by information, with the murder of Mr. James Wagner. He knowingly and willingly shot and killed Mr. Wagner." Judge Spencer asked the defense team if they had a response. Atty. Tom Broderick, "Not Guilty." Spencer set a trial date and an omnibus date for both sides to file their affirmative defenses.

Judge Spencer cited the severity of the charge before denying me a bond. After the court adjourned, a large contingent of deputies followed us from the courtroom. The media was close behind, constantly asking the defense team questions. I wondered why the court scheduled my court arraignment on the day of Wagner's funeral.

That evening on the ten o'clock news, a channel 8 WISH-TV news reporter showed a clip of my arraignment, then appeared live in front of a mall in Indianapolis. He walked up to attorney Patrick E. Chavis, III, and asked for his response to the murder charge against me in Anderson. Chavis replied, "My client has been under a lot of pressure lately; his life had been threatened."

Once I became an inmate at the Madison County detention center, the jail commander issued an order that inmates could no longer receive any newspapers. Several black deputies opined, "It prevents jailhouse snitches from concocting a story about you from those sources." Nevertheless, I was secretly provided with certain articles pertaining to me.

Friday, June 16, 1990, a day after the arraignment, a jail trustee showed me an Anderson Herald Bulletin newspaper. The headline read, "A GROUP OF PROMINENT CITIZENS MEET WITH CITY AND COUNTY OFFICIALS TO SUPPORT DR. VAN JOHNSON." The article noted that a group of very influential and prominent citizens met with city, county, and court officials in support of me. One citizen proclaimed on condition of anonymity, "Dr. Johnson would not harm a fly."

That Friday afternoon, my father, Sonja, and Liz, my sister, paid me a surprise visit at the county jail. However, jail officials didn't allow Liz in the visiting room. Jonathan didn't say anything. He sat there with his head down. Sonya told me that the Alpha's had planned several fundraisers for my defense fund. She said everybody we knew heard about the incident and was happy that I survived. But no one asked or mentioned the actual incident during this visit. Sonja pledged her full support. Three days later, I called Sonja from jail. She told me that Dr. Robert Lackey was waiting for them as they left the jail. He took them to his home where they had dinner and spent the evening. They received a lot of emotional support from the Lackeys.

The media portrayed Mr. James Wagner as this all-American family guy—a revered, little league baseball coach murdered in cold blood by a psychiatrist. However, there were several inmates at the jail who knew and presented a different profile of Wagner. Mr. John Fitzgerald, a middle-aged white man that lived in Elwood, proclaimed to be a fourth-generation Klansman from Giles County, Tennessee. Mr. Fitzgerald was in my cellblock, and we played card games. He interrupted our game to discuss my situation. "You're Dr. Van Johnson, a psychiatrist who treated a lot of white females from Elwood. You didn't know it, but they were the mothers, sisters, daughters, and wives of Klansmen. When the incident at your home was reported in the media, those women requested a special meeting with the Klan's top brass. They felt you sincerely wanted to help them and wanted our intervention to help you in return. We came to an agreement that if an investigation revealed you were corrupt, we'd let you hang. Richard Martz is your private investigator. His brother Larry is a high-ranking member of the Klan. Both of them went to investigate your background in Chicago. You have a clean record. The judge presiding over your case is one of our guys."

I couldn't hold it, "My judge is a Klansman?"

He replied, "He isn't the only judge around here in the Klan! Mr. Fitzgerald continued, "Me and a Klan enforcer named Mr. York met with Dr. Eugene Roach at a club called the Lucky Strike in Elwood. He was on the staff of St. John's hospital and wanted us to carry out a hit [sic] on you. Roach said the conflict was over a contract dispute. We told him that we were not going to kill a doctor over a legal dispute." Fitzgerald claimed that Mr. Wagner was having an affair with someone's wife, and they had a crew out searching for Wagner on the night of the shooting. "If they had caught up with Wagner earlier that night, that incident at your home would've never happened," he said. I mentioned being questioned by the jail commander about Wagner's missing wedding band. Fitzgerald said that Wagner's wedding band was located in a matchbox in the glove compartment of his car." Fitzgerald asked me to request his appearance at any hearing, to testify under oath.

One of my former hospital patients was placed in the cell block. I didn't initially recognize him. He started a conversation about the dubious publicity related to the incident at my home. I didn't want to discuss anything with him, but he claimed to have some information that may help my defense team. "Mr. Wagner lived several blocks from my home. The day after his death, I parked a block away and watched the activity at that home from a pair of binoculars. The late James Wagner must have had a special relationship with the Anderson police because their vehicles and those from other jurisdictions were parked around his home. I saw police carrying food and drink into their home." I asked if the Wagner home had any outstanding features that stood out? He replied, "They have an above-ground swimming pool in the backyard."

Mr. D. Gray was a young white man in his mid-twenties and claimed to be a brown belt in karate. He said, "James Wagner was a black belt in karate. I watched him perform in several contests. He was lightning-fast and lethal, as a well-polished black belt should be." He said that Wagner was barred from a tournament in Terre Haute, Indiana, but didn't know why. He ended the conversation by saying, "Hey Doc, you're lucky to be alive. He could've easily killed you with his bare hands or feet."

A week after my arrest, a young black man with an extensive criminal history named Trevor Nunn was released from the Pendleton Reformatory. On his way home, he killed a white woman that was disciplining her two biracial children for throwing rocks. He didn't know the woman. He was arrested and charged with murder. The Anderson Herald Bulletin newspaper placed a picture of me, next to one of him, on the front page with the following headline, "BLACKS KILLING WHITES IN MADISON COUNTY." I had never met Mr. Nunn. In essence, my case was being tried in the media. In the interest of justice, the court should've instituted a gag order on my case. The headline insinuated that the two homicides were linked and racially motivated.

On Friday, June 22, 1990, they held another court hearing, but this time, in their largest courtroom. The crowd consisted of well-dressed white folks, elected officials, and prominent community leaders. When Judge Spencer brought the court to session, Chavis rose and said, "Judge, my client was insane at the time of the shooting, and he is insane now. He's unable to assist us in his defense. Please, just listen to him, and you will see what I am talking about!" He sat down and whispered in my ear, "All information enters the court through various corridors. I want you to get up there and tell those people everything that others have told you, and what happened to you since coming to this town. This will be your only opportunity to tell that story." The judge had a deputy escort me in front of the audience.

I first expressed remorse to the Wagner family and made it clear that I never met James Wagner, his wife, and didn't know their children delivered my newspapers. I presented in elaborate detail how St. John's Hospital fraudulently recruited me to come there and then breached numerous contractual agreements. I mentioned the aborted meeting with Mr. Stevens and the reason they supposedly lured me to Anderson. They heard about the vandalism to my car, late-night phone threats, and the morning when my office was burglarized. I told them about the barmaid who disclosed the police surveillance of me, my patient who mentioned my name broadcasted over the sheriff's radio, and the state trooper who warned me about the contract on my life. The crowded courtroom sat totally silent as I mentioned the meeting between Mr. John Fitzgerald and Dr. Eugene Roach for the purpose of soliciting a Ku Klux Klan hit on me.

A guard escorted me back to my seat after the lengthy presentation. Chavis leaned over and whispered, "You did an excellent job." After a long period of silence in the courtroom, Judge Spencer proclaimed the law of the court. "Dr. Van Johnson is not insane. He is very articulate, intelligent, and well-educated. I will leave the question of his competency to stand trial with those trained in that field." This meant that the court would only entertain the issue of me being competent to stand trial. The judge instructed the defense team to file their affirmative defenses before an Omnibus date, and then set the trial date for ninety days from that hearing.

The prosecutor stated, "Dr. Johnson is very articulate and refined. For that reason, we can't allow him in front of any television cameras, or radio microphones. Judge, he should be gagged!" The judge made no ruling on their floor motion.

As I sat in the county jail awaiting trial, the local newspaper ran daily front-page stories about me gathered from rumors, innuendos, and leaked information from the police. One article begged the question, "Why would a black man listen to music by Glen Campbell, Black Sabbath, the Righteous Brothers, Blue Oyster Cult, Led Zeppelin, the Cars, Strawberry Alarm Clock, and Frank Sinatra?" The article failed to mention that white folks love music by black artists. As a matter of fact, white folks purchase more rap music than blacks. One of the reporters for the town's only newspaper penned an article that insinuated that I had an affinity for black magic and the occult. Police revealed that in my library there were several masonic bibles, a book on the history of the occult, and a book titled *God, Man, and the Thinker*. This was an attempt to alienate the sympathies of the religious community. Police claimed they found pornography in my home. There were a few copies of *Player* magazine on top of the bookshelves—an out of sight location. It was a popular magazine with professional blacks, similar in format to *Playboy* magazine.

The defense team filed the affirmative defenses of "Self Defense," mistake of fact, and voluntary intoxication prior to the omnibus deadline.

In September 1990, I underwent a psychiatric evaluation at Winona Hospital in Indianapolis. It was conducted by Dr. Randy May. I met him after becoming the medical director of Mid-America consultants. (Dr. May was a native of Bowling Green, KY. and heard about me when I practiced at Cumberland Hall in Hopkinsville, KY.) Dr. May expressed deep sadness at my situation. "Dr. Johnson, the hospital board was in the process of accepting your application for staff privileges," he said. I explained in full detail what happened at my home that led to the shooting.

Several weeks later, there was another court hearing. Judge Spencer mentioned that the defense had filed their affirmative defenses and spoke briefly about the upcoming trial. Spencer asked Nave, the deputy prosecutor, and the defense team if there was anything either side wanted to discuss. Chavis requested permission to interpose a belated insanity defense. Mr. James Nave, the chief deputy prosecutor, objected because the omnibus deadline had passed. Judge Spencer asked Chavis, "Why did you not file that motion prior to the omnibus date?" Chavis replied, "Your honor, no psychiatrist or mental health specialist in Madison County would get involved with this case." Chavis presented Dr. Randy May's evaluation to the judge, but he only allowed the chief deputy prosecutor to only visually examine Dr. Strain's report, citing confidentiality between doctor and patient. When Spencer reviewed Dr. Strain's report, he canceled the trial date.

In March 1991, Dr. Randy May testified about my psychiatric evaluation during a court hearing. Dr. May told the court, "Dr. Johnson suffered from a rare paranoid delusional syndrome. He was insane at the time of the shooting." Most people don't know it, but psychiatrists very rarely give black folks the diagnosis of being "insane at the time of a crime!" His presentation lasted well over an hour and included graphs, statistics, and excerpts from psychiatry textbooks projected on a large screen in the courtroom. The legal definition of insanity is handled quite differently from the way it is handled in a hospital. Even though the defense of Insanity is rarely successful in courts, it could be used as a corridor to allow certain information before the court. Despite his diagnosis, I was never hospitalized or placed on any medication. The judge had already ruled that I was sane! Dr. May's evaluation could only be used as a tool to delay the trial.

When Dr. May concluded his presentation, James Nave, chief deputy prosecutor, objected with supporting case law, to the insanity defense at trial. Spencer then postponed the trial indefinitely, as the matter would be taken under advisement. The case law stipulated that Judge Spencer had the discretion to wait a day before trial, to rule on that motion to interpose the insanity defense. The belated filing put the ball squarely in

Spencer's court and gave him a constitutional reason for delaying the trial, which allowed a cooling-off period, and new facts to emerge in the case. If Chavis had filed the motion before the omnibus date, the state would've countered by having me evaluated by three psychiatrists. If they had ruled that I was psychotic (insane), the state would've moved the court to have me committed to a psychiatric facility—most likely, for the rest of my life.

Before the session was adjourned, Spencer addressed another matter. "I will not allow self-defense to be used as a jury instruction at trial. Dr. Johnson, you don't have a corroborating eyewitness to support your claim that Wagner attacked you!" Without the ability to invoke the defense of self-defense, the insanity defense was the only other way a defendant could be allowed to speak about their state of mind at the time of the shooting to a jury. Without either defense, the court wouldn't allow testimony about the influences that shaped my percep-tions! They would be disallowed under the hearsay rule. I thought the Defense was allowed to use any defense it saw appropriate. I wondered if blacks were prohibited from invoking the Second Amendment right to self-defense, when it came to white assailants. Once the hearing was adjourned, Chavis said, "Dr. Johnson, your color is the problem! If you came home and killed Wagner while he was raping Sonja, you would be facing the same drama. None of the white citizens in this town believe that Wagner did what you claimed!"

Now that the defense team had some breathing room, Chavis assigned each member a role. He and Broderick would conduct all mat-ters of litigation. Oliver would act solely in a fiduciary capacity to pay my bills from a trust fund.

Darnell Johnson, my half-brother, was a forensic specialist in upstate New York. He came to Anderson to visit me at the jail. He hap-pened to stop by Oliver's law office (an abandoned Clark service station, converted into an office with living quarters). When he knocked, a white woman answered the door and said Oliver was not available. Darnell left, but had a hunch that Oliver was in that office. He waited in a restaurant across the street for about thirty minutes, and then returned. This time the woman allowed him inside. She disappeared into a room. Darnell browsed around and noticed a door to a room was ajar. He looked inside and noticed my jewelry box on top of a dresser, and my Sony stereo system in the corner. He knew it was mine because we chipped the upper corner of the glass door putting the stack system together; a flaw that stood out like a sore thumb, so to speak.

Darnell said Oliver emerged from the back room clad in a bath robe. His eyes were bloodshot, and a white powder covered his nostrils and mustache. Since there was no food on Oliver's face, Darnell thought that the white powder was cocaine. He declined Oliver's request to take over the responsibility of paying my monthly car note. When Darnell arrived at the jail, he asked me, "Why did you hire a dope fiend for your lawyer?" Then he described the scene at Oliver's office. When my brother left the jail, I filed a "Pro Se" motion to dismiss Attorney Oliver as counsel. The jail commander refused to notarize the document. Later that afternoon, all three lawyers came to the jail. Chavis led the discussion. "It would not be a good idea to dismiss Attorney Oliver." Attorney Broderick added, "You have too much working against you in this town. Any negative thing in the newspaper would only hurt you. If you dismiss Atty. Oliver, I will also withdraw my representation." Chavis again explained the importance of having a former white chief deputy prosecutor of that town on my defense team.

I replied, "Oliver doesn't represent my interest. I believe he's a double agent operating to sabotage my defense." Pat told Oliver to be more responsive and reliable. Just months later, Chavis paid a visit to the jail, but this time he appeared sad and spoke softly with his head down. "Atty. Oliver has just fucked up this case." He wouldn't tell me what Oliver had done. I ordered Chavis to immediately fire Oliver. But Chavis replied, "I can't fire him!" He wouldn't say why.

In June 1991, my father and Irvin, his brother, paid a visit to me in jail. They were well-dressed and, on their way, to have dinner with Reverend Leo Scaife Sr., their first cousin. Rev Leo was patriarch of the Scaife family, senior pastor of Union Baptist Church in Muncie, Indiana. After their meeting, the Scaife family began making weekend visits to the jail in Anderson. There were so many of them, I couldn't remember names with faces. I didn't expect anything from my father. He rarely wrote and never sent financial support. Six months after his visit, the jail announced that I had an attorney visit. When the first-floor elevator doors opened, Chavis, Broderick, Oliver, the jail commander, and the sheriff were standing there waiting. Chavis walked up to me, "Your father died last night in his sleep. I'm sorry for your loss." Everyone in the group expressed their condolences. Rev. Mel Goode, the pastor of the Sherman Street Church of God came to the jail and had a prayer session with me later that afternoon. When I notified Dr. Lackey about my father's passing, he said, "It would be impossible for me to visit you in that jail. I couldn't handle seeing a dear friend locked up!"

Judge Spencer held an emergency hearing to determine if it was possible for me to attend my father's funeral. Spencer gave his condolences and then said, "I see no issue with him attending the funeral; release him to the sheriff." However, the sheriff mandated certain stipulations. I had to pay for the cost of travel and lodging for my escort of deputies. Since my father's funeral was scheduled for that upcoming weekend, the sheriff and jail commander promised to meet with me that Thursday to discuss the travel plans. On Thursday, I became suspicious when guards in the control booth kept telling me the commander was unavailable. This occurred throughout the weekend. Of course, I missed my father's funeral.

On Monday morning, the jail commander had me brought to her office. When I entered, she asked, "How was your father's funeral?"

I responded, "You know Goddamn well I didn't go to any funeral. Why would you bring me here to insult my intelligence?" She turned red-faced and ordered a guard to take me back to the cell block.

Several black sheriff deputies confided with me. They had volunteered to transport me to Chicago without any financial stipulations. The sheriff and jail commander cited security concerns and blocked their request.

The jail staff notified me that an article appeared in the Chicago Defender newspaper about me not being at my father's funeral. "Black

Doctor Denied Attendance to his Father's Funeral." On August 1, 1990, Dr. Conrad Worrill penned a one-page article about my dilemma called "The Dr. Van Johnson Case," in the Chicago Defender Newspaper.

12   CHICAGO DEFENDER - Wednesday, August 1, 1990

Worrill's World

The Dr. Van Johnson case

by Dr. Conrad W. Worrill

(Dr. Worrill is the national chairman of the National Black United Front (NBUF), located at 700 E. Oakwood Blvd., Chicago, IL 60653, (312) 268-7500 x154.)

Throughout the years African Americans have been present in this country, there have been countless times that they were unjustly charged and convicted by the white-dominated criminal justice system.

Another such case appears to be emerging. On June 10, 1990, Dr. Van Johnson, who was living and practicing psychiatry in Anderson, Ind. from all reports we have received, accidentally shot a white man, James Wagner, 44, who apparently was prowling around this property.

Anderson, Ind. is a small, predominantly white town about 250 miles from Chicago. Dr. Johnson moved to Anderson to set up his practice in July of 1989. During the year that Dr. Johnson has lived and worked in Anderson, he reported to his family and friends in Chicago that there was strong resentment by the white community against him setting up his psychiatry practice in the town. He had been harassed on numerous occasions and, in fact, his life had been threatened, as well as his property.

Apparently, some of the white people in Anderson were upset because Dr. Johnson was treating white patients and had a white secretary. His practice seemed to be developing quite well, which caused even more resentment on the part of some whites in the town.

According to Dr. Johnson's statements, on "Sunday, June 10, 1990, Dr. Johnson heard strange noises followed by a shadow figure darting outside his windows and front door of this home. He called out for the person to identify himself and there was no response. In fear for his life, and personal possessions, he secured his shotgun to protect himself and frighten the prowler away."

Dr. Johnson goes on to state that "when he opened his door, the weapon accidentally discharged and the apparent figure he had seen darting outside his windows fell forward."

At this point, Dr. Johnson explains he tried to identify the victim and attempted to save his life through resuscitation. When it was apparent he could not revive the man through resuscitation, Dr. Johnson called the police. The victim died on the scene.

According to news accounts, "Dr. Johnson was held for formal questioning and on Monday, June 11, 1990, the police received court approval to hold him in jail for 72 hours pending the conclusion of the preliminary investigation to determine if the shooting was accidental or whether he should be charged."

In the meantime, Dr. Johnson announced on Wednesday, June 13, 1990, that he was willing "to surrender all of his financial assets to the deceased man's widow."

Anderson police reported that the deceased was "James Wagner, a 44-year-old mechanical engineer who they claim went to Johnson's home to collect money for his son's paper route."

On Tuesday, June 12, 1990, Dr. Johnson's assets were frozen by a court order as a result of a civil suit filed against him by the wife of the deceased.

Two days later, June 14, a hearing was held and he was charged with first degree murder. Isn't it interesting that the court would freeze his assets, making it difficult for him to secure a lawyer of his choosing, and then charge him with first degree murder?

Dr. Johnson, who is 38 years old, was born and raised in Chicago and graduated from Von Steuben High School Science Center and the University of Illinois, Chicago campus in 1975. In 1981, Dr. Johnson graduated from Rush Presbyterian St. Luke's Medical School and completed his internship at Mt. Sinai Hospital and his psychiatry residence at the Illinois State Psychiatric Institute.

In his fast-growing practice in Anderson, more than 85 percent of Dr. Johnson's clients were white and it was rumored that he was taking business from the other white doctors in the town and that they were becoming quite upset with his success.

Additionally, Dr. Johnson was the first African American psychiatrist to set up a practice in the history of Madison County, Ind.

In my judgment, this appears to be classic case of a Black man accidentally shooting a white man in a predominantly white town. Then, all the white power forces in the town come together to insure that revenge takes place regardless of the law or justice.

The African American community has a responsibility to support and protect our people wherever they are, particularly in situations of this nature. Dr. Van Johnson deserves our support and we must prevent another miscarriage of justice against an African American who is obviously a victim of circumstances.

Washington Window

Then, *The Burning Spear,* posted an article called "African Doctor Railroaded." In that article, James Wagner was labeled a Klansman. The *Tri-State Tribune* published an article called "A Legal Lynching."

85

Two months prior to my trial, the defense team filed a motion for bond. I understood that the court didn't want any surprises. During that hearing, Mrs. Duvall, a retired educator, lived next door to me. She took the stand and said, "James Wagner came to my home around noontime on that Sunday to collect for the newspaper. I had no small change and offered him a fifty-dollar bill. He refused and said, 'Just hold on to your money because I won't be back in this area today.' Atty. Broderick commented, "I guess it took him over nine hours to walk next door to Dr. Johnson's home." Ironically, at trial, the defense team didn't subpoena her to testify. I viewed this as evidence they sold me out. Her testimony would've cast serious doubts about the media alibi given to Wagner for being in that neighborhood at night.

Chavis was the only defense attorney who ever mentioned reviewing the state's evidence with me. He said every time he asked Nave, deputy chief prosecutor, for the state's pictorial evidence and crime scene videotape, Nave always said that Star China hadn't developed it yet.

I knew that Broderick and Oliver were acting as double agents for the power-to-be in Anderson. White supremacy wanted to control both sides of the debate. Both lawyers carried heavy political debts and dirty baggage: Broderick had to resign as the deputy chief prosecutor of Madison County after a DUI arrest. His upcoming trial was scheduled to take place after he helped the state remove me from society. Nave was his former employee. I believe Broderick knew that police had altered the state's evidence in my home. He lied to me with a straight face. "The most important evidence in this case is your statement to the police." As a former prosecutor, he knew damn well that the "objective evidence," i.e., crime scene video and photographic evidence, is the most compelling evidence in a trial. He could've gotten that evidence from Nave, his former employee and friend, with just a phone call. He was in collusion with local officials. The reason for denying me an examination of the state's evidence before trial? My defense team knew that I married a former congressional candidate and well-connected in Chicago. They knew that if I saw how police changed and altered evidence in my home, it would've been exposed in the black media of Chicago. Once the U. S. The Department of Justice and FBI got involved, their case would've been severely compromised, if not thrown out altogether for prosecutorial misconduct.

Chapter Five

A WEEK PRIOR TO TRIAL, SPENCER HELD A COURT HEARING. HE denied Chavis' motion to interpose the insanity defense. Attys Chavis and Broderick then withdrew the motion. Spencer also denied their motion to "In Limine" (to deny prejudicial or illegal testimony) two witnesses for the state. Sherry Ganger and Lathan were state witnesses that were going to testify at trial about the "fire extinguisher" incident. Defense attorneys argued that their testimony would violate Indiana Trial Rule 404(b). Their testimonies were meant to augment the state's theory that I was "inherently criminal." Spencer did approve a defense motion that prevented me from being seen in leg shackles, handcuffs, or in jail clothing at trial. The defense motion to have me classified as indigent brought an objection by Atty. James Nave, deputy chief prosecutor, who also accused me of grossly undervaluing my assets. Judge Spencer overruled him and granted indigency status to me. The court appointed Oliver as my appellate counsel on direct appeal and released $750 dollars for me to purchase clothing for trial.

Broderick and a deputy transported me to a high-end clothing store where he picked out my attire for trial. Broderick was one of the best dress lawyers in that courthouse.

On May 22, 1990, my murder trial commenced in the Madison County courthouse. My defense team and I marched into a courtroom packed with angry white folks. As I looked into the crowd, all I saw were angry white faces that reminded of an old fashion lynch mob. Not one member of my family or fraternity was present in that court room throughout the trial. Chavis mentioned how the lack of family and friends affects the jury's perception of a person.

After the court was brought to the session, William Lawler, the county prosecutor, read the criminal indictment and then the court proceeded to the "Voir dire" phase of trial. It supposedly flushes out bias or prejudice in potential jurors. The goal for the defense is to eliminate jurors that would be biased towards me. Each side has ten chances to strike someone from the panel. However, only four strikes were used, and they were all natives of Anderson. The final jury panel consisted of ten jurors from Elwood, one from the town of Alexandria, and the only black was a twenty-one-year-old female from the Pine Tree housing project in Anderson. After jurors chose their foreman, they were sworn in.

Atty. James Nave presented the opening statement. "This case will only be tried once! The evidence during this trial will prove that Dr. Van Johnson is inherently a criminal. He is a self-made man. Despite his refinement and privileged education, underneath that skin is a hardened criminal from Chicago. The late James Wagner disturbed his leisure, and that was the motive for the shooting."

Lt. Richwine, chief detective for the Anderson police, was the state's first witness. The highlight of his testimony. "Dr. Johnson told me that he noticed a white man staring through his bedroom window." At the cross, defense Atty. Broderick handed Richwine a black folder that contained his official report. He asked Det. Richwine to read the report out loud. Richwine examined the document for several minutes, his face turned red, but he remained silent. After several minutes of agonizing embarrassment, Broderick excused him from the witness stand. The red-faced detective slowly rose from his seat to exit the courtroom. Once out of the courtroom, Atty. Broderick told the jury, "Not one time did Dr. Johnson describe the late Mr. James Wagner in racial terms."

The next person to take the stand was a neighbor who I had never met. She was a defense witness. An attractive, married white woman with two sons. Her family lived a short distance from my home. She testified that at approximately 8:38 p.m. on the night of the shooting, one of her boys ran to warn her that someone was staring through their kitchen window. Her husband was upset and opened their door to find Wagner walking away in a hurry. Wagner claimed to be collecting newspaper debt. Her husband asked Wagner to send them a bill and not to come there again. According to her, Wagner was dressed in a light-colored shirt, blue jeans, and white gym shoes.

Anderson police technician said that I had gunpowder residue on my hand in my home and that I admitted to shooting James Wagner. He said Wagner had no powder residue on his light-colored shirt or the underlying skin! (Lt. Richwine told a reporter that Wagner was shot at "point-blank range" during an interview with channel 8 WISH-TV.) That is inconsistent with someone shot at point-blank range!

A police firearm specialist described the shotgun shell that killed Wagner as a number four green-sleeve shell. It's usually used to kill small rodents around the yard. Because of the distance from where it was fired, the pellets didn't have a chance to spread further apart.

An investigator took the stand. "Dr. Van Johnson has no previous misdemeanor or felony convictions. His blood alcohol level was 0.22mg percent, five hours after arrest. If we were dealing with true justice, the investigator would've disclosed if James Wagner had any previous misdemeanor or felony convictions. His blood toxicology report would've been revealed.

Lawler, the county prosecutor, showed the court on the big screen, a ball jar liter of Moonshine police had taken from my kitchen pantry. It was a souvenir from Dr. Winston, who had a copper still in his basement. Why didn't they show pictures of my well stocked bar in the den?

The publisher of the Anderson Herald Bulletin newspaper was subpoenaed as a defense witness. Atty. Broderick conducted the direct. "Does your business have a handbook that governs the times and days employees collect for the newspaper?"

The publisher responded, "No. We leave that to the people who run the routes."

Atty. Broderick then asked, "So there's no structure to the operations?"

The publisher responded, "Some of the people that distribute and collect are subcontractors and operate at their own discretion."

Atty. Broderick next asked, "Were the Wagner's your employees?"

The publisher answered, "I think they were subcontractors."

Atty. Broderick queried, "How much did Dr. Johnson owe on his bill?"

"I don't know."

Ironically, every article published in his newspaper claimed that Wagner was at my home to collect newspaper debt. But now he can't disclose the amount of debt I owed? Did I owe a debt? Or did they just claim it to give Wagner an alibi for being at my home? What was the real reason for Wagner coming to my home?

Mrs. Jan Wagner, the decedent's wife, took the witness stand. Atty. Nave conducted the direct, Atty. Broderick conducted the cross.

On direct, Nave asked. "Mrs. Wagner, could you describe your marriage to the late James Wagner?"

"We have three children, and one daughter has a heart condition. We got the paper route so the children could learn responsibility. It was a family project. James and I got divorced and remarried." (She said nothing about the quality of their marriage. Since the paper route was a family project, why didn't she tell the court what I owed for the newspaper? She heard the publisher say that he didn't know. Why couldn't someone tell the court what I owed?)

Atty. Nave then asked, "Mrs. Wagner, please describe the evening of the tragic event."

"James left home around 7:20 p.m. It worried me when he did not come home within a few hours. Someone called and asked if James was all right. That is when I drove down the state road, Route 105, and saw the police cars and ambulance at the Crosslake apartment complex. A police officer told me that my husband was fatally wounded."

I wondered why Broderick did not ask Mrs. Wagner this simple question. "Mrs. Wagner, did you notice anything unusual when you identified your husband's body in Dr. Johnson's home?" She told police her husband's wedding band was missing when she identified the body! It was the reason the police were granted a search warrant to search my home. How does a former prosecutor miss that red flag?

Atty. Broderick continued his cross. "Mrs. Wagner, have you ever met Dr. Johnson?"

"When he first moved there, the family went to the apartment to solicit a subscription."

Atty. Broderick then asked, "Was there ever a conflict between him and any member of your family?"

"No there was not. But Dr. Johnson would have shot anyone that came to his home that night." Ironically, her daughter testified at a bond hearing, that I gave her a five-dollar tip during the Christmas holiday. The state did not subpoena the child to testify at trial.

A police investigator testified that they towed my car to the pound and searched it. Atty. Broderick asked, "Where was Mr. Wagner's car parked?"

Police replied, "Parked next to Dr. Johnson's car in the driveway."

"Why didn't you tow his car away and search it as well?"

"We allowed someone to drive Wagner's car back to their home. Several hours later, an officer went to their home and shined a flashlight through Wagner's car windows, and nothing appeared suspicious." (According to court transcripts, the wife of an Anderson police officer name R. Knuckles, drove Mr. Wagner's car away from my home. She aided in the disposal of key evidence obtained from my home.)

The court played my forty-minute recorded statement to police on the night of the shooting. I described all my mistreatments and threats received during my life in Anderson—albeit interspersed with hiccups, including a loud one at the end, which ignited roaring laughter from the audience.

After a lunch break, Broderick put the police officer who arrested me on the witness stand. "Why wasn't Dr. Johnson immediately taken to the hospital for the toxicology blood test?"

The officer did not answer Broderick's question."

"You put Dr. Johnson in an isolation room for five hours, because he said that he had several beers. You were hoping his blood-alcohol level would return to zero during that period," said Atty. Broderick. He

THE LEGAL LYNCHING OF A BLACK PSYCHIATRIST

continued, "If you had stopped Dr. Johnson while he was driving, you would've arrested him for DUI."

The officer replied, "I don't think so!"

Alcohol intoxication is a legal defense, but the person must be so drunk that they could not produce intent. However, it has been shown to produce a diminished capacity at the time of a homicide. The court foreclosed the defense of self-defense because no white person in that town believed Wagner attacked me. The jury had to be given other explanations to consider why I did not knowingly or willfully kill Mr. Wagner.

A toxicologist from Purdue University took the witness stand for the defense. He first informed the court about the different firearms he owned. His lecture was on how alcohol affected a person's judgment, perception, and reflexes. Because the Anderson police waited five hours before taking me to have my blood drawn at the hospital, he used a 'reverse progression' formula to determine my blood alcohol level at the time of the shooting. That level of alcohol was calculated to be 0.297 mg percent. He showed a chart that compared blood-alcohol levels to perceptual, physiological, and cognitive alterations. On a large screen, there was an image of a human casket next to blood alcohol levels of 0.4 mg percent and above. Statistically, over eighty percent of people died with that level or above.

According to his calculations, my blood-alcohol level would've significantly impaired anyone's decisions, coordination, and judgment. He ended the presentation with a question directed at himself, "Would I go to answer the door with a gun in my hand?" Then answered his own question, "I would under suspicious circumstances." It left the packed courtroom in complete silence.

Immediately after the lecture, Atty. Broderick moved for withdrawal of the Voluntary Intoxication Defense, saying, "It would put my client in grave peril." I now understood what Chavis meant by certain defenses allowing information before the court. Nave concurred with Broderick's move to withdraw the defense of voluntary intoxication by saying, "Dr. Johnson's level of intoxication did not impair his ability to call a lawyer, attempt CPR on the wounded man, or call 911 ten minutes after the shooting."

Ms. Vera Dupree, the Indiana state trooper, took the witness stand for the defense. Atty. Chavis conducted the direct exam. He started by asking about her present situation. Vera identified herself as a state police officer on a leave of absence and under treatment with antidepressant medication. Atty. Chavis, "Have you ever called Dr. Johnson's home?"

"Yes."

"Did you ever make a visit to his home?"

"Yes."

"How long did the visit last?"

Vera answered, "I was there well over two hours."

Atty. Chavis commented, "That was time for a lot of conversation." Chavis, "What was the nature of that visit?"

Before she could respond, the prosecutor and his deputy objected and disrupted the proceedings. "Whatever she discloses is hearsay," said Nave. Judge Spencer ordered the jury to leave the courtroom for a side-bar. This occurred at least eleven times during the twenty-five minutes that she was on the witness stand. The prosecutor went as far as to ask Atty. Chavis, "What are you going to ask her next?" It was humiliating to see her treated with such disrespect. Whenever Atty. Chavis asked a question, the prosecutors responded with objections. Atty. Chavis was so frustrated that he asked the judge to order the state to allow his witness to answer pertinent questions. When that did not occur, he excused Ms. Dupree from the witness stand and said, "The state won't allow her to answer any questions." The state waived cross-examination.

The vice-president of General Motors was a defense witness. He was my next-door neighbor and supervised all seventeen GM factories in Anderson. Atty. Broderick on direct asked, "Was the music from Dr. Johnson's apartment ever loud enough to be heard?"

"No!"

"Were police ever at his home for any domestic disturbances?"

"No!"

Atty. Broderick then asked, "Have you ever met Dr. Johnson?"

This time, the vice president responded at length. "No. But, he was well-dressed and groomed whenever I saw him. I often saw him carry his laundry and dry-cleaned clothes into his apartment."

Atty. Broderick queried, "How would you rate Dr. Johnson as a neighbor?"

"He was an ideal neighbor," the V.P. replied.

The retired chief of Anderson's fire department was the last defense witness to take the stand. Prior to taking the stand and being sworn in, he loudly announced that he witnessed the whole incident. He lived in the apartment complex, but I had never met or seen him before.

Atty. Broderick on direct, "Did you see or hear anything unusual on the Sunday night of June 10, 1990?"

The fire chief answered, "I heard a loud bang, looked at my clock, and ran outside. I knew the noise came from a firearm in the area where Dr. Johnson lived. I went outside to investigate, but did not see anyone near, or in front of his home."

"What time did you hear the gunshot?"

"My clock showed 9:00 p.m."

"How much of Dr. Johnson's apartment can you see from your apartment?"

The fire chief answered, "I have a direct view of his patio and the front door of his apartment."

Atty. Broderick asked, "Did you see anything on his patio?"

"I didn't see anything or anyone on the patio."

Finally, Atty. Broderick asked, "Have you ever met Dr. Johnson?"

"I know him by sight, but never met him personally," the fire chief said.

Bill Lawler, the prosecutor, disputed the time when the fire chief claimed he heard the gunshot. The state brought in the two witnesses to testify about the so-called "fire-extinguisher" incident at my home. The court denied a defense motion to 'In Limine' their testimony. Atty. Broderick informed the court of his continuing objection.

The first witness was Sherry Granger. Atty. Nave conducted the direct examination. He asked her to describe what happened when she and a co-worker visited my home to inspect a fire extinguisher.

Granger started, "We went to his home at 1:30 p.m. and knocked on the door. When no one answered, we opened the door with a passkey, but the safety latch was engaged. Dr. Johnson opened the door holding a large silver .45 caliber pistol, like the one they used in the movie Dirty Harry. He pointed the gun at my heart and said, 'I could kill you.' It frightened me and I feared for my life.'"

Atty. Nave asked, "Did he allow you into the apartment to check the fire extinguisher?"

"Yes. He allowed us in to do our job."

Attorney Broderick objected, "I want to remind the court of my continuing objection to her testimony." On cross, "If you feared for your life, why did you go into his home?" She did not answer the question. Atty. Broderick continued, "Were you wearing some type of uniform?"

"I was wearing street clothes," she answered.

"Did you have any identification?"

"No," she said.

When Attorney Broderick asked if she saw the extensive damage done to the doorframe, she said management had the damage repaired. Attorney Broderick asked, "Did you make a complaint about the incident?"

"I reported it to management," she replied.

"Did you complain about it to anyone else?"

"I also reported the incident to Lt. Richwine of the Anderson police department," she said.

"I'm going to ask you one last question. Are you sure no one else was in that home when this happened?"

Her face reddened, "There was no one else in that house," she replied.

Atty. Broderick asked, "Did you go into every room in that home?"

"Yes," she said.

Once she left the courtroom, Broderick gave the jurors an enlarged photo of my Glock 9mm black handgun to examine. He explained to the jurors that if my conduct was illegal, the Anderson police would have pressed charges against me.

Mr. Latham, the man that was with Granger that day, took the witness stand. He was a tall stocky white man that was in his early forties. Atty. Nave asked him to describe the incident at my home. He gave a different narrative, "We went to Dr. Johnson's home and damaged his door by forcing entry against the safety latch. He never pointed the gun at me. I never felt at any time afraid in his presence. That guy would not hurt anybody. We were dressed in street clothes with no identification".

Atty. Broderick on the cross asked, "Who repaired his door?"

He replied, "I think the management."

The defense team subpoenaed the property manager of Crosslake Apartments to testify about the fire extinguisher incident. Atty. Broderick asked, "Did you ever have a problem with Dr. Johnson?"

The manager answered, "He paid the rent on time and police were never called to his place."

"Did you get a complaint from several people about Dr. Johnson when they went to his apartment to inspect the fire extinguisher?"

"Yes. The woman said he came to the door with a gun and pointed it at her."

"Did you ever notify Dr. Johnson about the complaint to get his side of the story?"

"No," she replied.

Atty. Broderick asked, "Why didn't you?" She held her red face down and never answered his question. Atty. Broderick continued, "Did you notify the police about the incident?"

She said, "I didn't notify police, but warned other residents and anyone that would come into contact with him, to be very careful."

"Did that include the Wagner family?"

She replied, "Especially them, because of their children."

The state waived cross-exam.

After a lunch break, the state and defense team huddled together with the crime scene photographs; the ones they never showed me. They gave them to the jury. Afterwards, they moved the state to enter the items as evidence—and without any review of that evidence from me. The court played the crime scene videotape to the jury on a 19-inch television. However, they set the television for only the jury to see. After the jurors viewed the videotape, some had a strange look on their faces. It was expressions I could not read.

The state medical examiner (M.E.) at Indiana University performed a forensic autopsy on Wagner. Broderick conducted the cross. On the witness stand, the M.E. first described Wagner's injuries. "I received the body of the late James Wagner from the coroner of Madison County. There was no gunpowder residue on the decedent's shirt, skin, or wound. The shot pellets entered from a downward to an upward direction through the chest cavity. They transected the thoracic aorta, vein, and esophagus with direct damage to the heart.

Attorney Broderick on cross. "In your estimate, how long did he live after being shot?"

"Approximately seventeen seconds."

"So, he didn't suffer long."

The medical examiner replied, "That's fair to say."

"No more questioning." Why did Broderick end the cross-examination without asking about Wagner's toxicology profile? As a former prosecutor, he knew that toxicology profiles were mandatory in homicides. The medical examiner was a witness for the state. I believe that if Wagner's blood was clean, the results would've been disclosed spontaneously! (During an interview with WISH-TV, Lt. Richwine said that Wagner was shot at point blank range, which would contradict the lack of gunpowder residue on Wagner's shirt and skin!

Here is my theory about Broderick's conduct. Asking about the toxicology profile could have potentially exposed the coverup by the Madison County medical examiner. It would've taken place prior to its transfer to I.U. university – Wagner's blood could have been replaced by embalming fluid to prevent the detection of drugs or alcohol. If Broderick had asked for the toxicology profile and it was positive for illegal drugs, the Jury would have acquitted me out right.

After two weeks of trial, the state and defense were ready to present their respective closing arguments. The state had the burden of proving guilt and allowed to present its argument first; allowed a rebuttal after the defense presented its argument.

Atty. James Nave presented the state's closing argument. "Dr. Van Johnson is a very polished and educated man, but innately criminal from his days in Chicago. Mr. James Wagner came to his home in an attempt to collect for his son's paper route. When he knocked on the door, Dr. Johnson opened it, and fatally shot him. Then he attempted to hide what happened by dragging Wagner's body into his home. Dr. Johnson was not drunk at the time of the shooting. In fact, there was no alcohol in his bloodstream at the time of the shooting. After the shooting, his guilty conscience took over. He knew that being intoxicated at the time of the shooting could result in acquittal for criminal liability. With a hard-earned career on the line, Dr. Johnson went to his bar in the den and drank eighteen shots of scotch whisky within ten minutes. That is what raised his blood alcohol to those levels of intoxication. Mr. Wagner simply disturbed his leisure, which is the motive behind the shooting. There is no proof that Wagner attacked him. The police found no fingerprints on any windows. Dr. Johnson called his lawyer prior to calling 911."

In my statement to the police, they asked if Wagner entered the home. I said, "No. I did not allow him inside my home. He rushed me when I opened the door." I told them that I dragged Wagner's body into my living room. It had the only source of light to assess his injuries and attempt CPR. The latter was confirmed by Nave during his debate against the jury instruction on Voluntary intoxication. Furthermore, I never claimed that Wagner touched a window, or tried to enter my home through a window.

Atty Thomas Broderick, Jr., presented the closing argument for the defense. "Ladies and gentlemen of the jury, this was indeed a tragedy. However, not all homicides are the result of criminal intent. Dr. Johnson was where he was supposed to be that night. Dr. Johnson and the Wagner family were not enemies. If they had a conflict, you would have heard about it from his wife. You all heard Dr. Johnson's lengthy statement to the police. He did not mislead anyone about what happened on the night of the shooting. He told how he brought Mr. Wagner in from the cold, and what type of CPR he tried to administer. If he was incorrect, the state would have had a doctor in here to contradict him. Dr. Johnson did not try to mop up the pool of blood at the door breach. He did not place a weapon in Wagner's hand. This is what happened, Wagner was in a big hurry. He walked off the patio but heard the door open and ran back from the blind side of the patio and suddenly appeared in front of Dr. Johnson. What happened was a tragic accident and no more."

Atty. Nave on rebuttal added, "When Mr. Wagner charged at Dr. Johnson, he was trying to disarm him."

Judge Spencer made a declaration after both sides rested their cases. "There's no evidence whatsoever of self-defense in this case!" He instructed jurors not to discuss the case with neighbors, family, or friends. The jury received instructions on the elements of murder, mistake of fact, or the verdict of "not guilty". Then sent the jury to deliberate a verdict.

During the two weeks of deliberations, a thunderstorm caused the courtroom to be evacuated one evening. During that process, the jury had to be moved to the basement of the courthouse. However, defense attorneys noticed the Wagner family in the same elevator as the jury. They observed jurors offering the Wagner family food and blankets; and expressing condolences to them. When the court went back to session, Atty. Broderick moved the court for a mistrial. The improper interaction between the Wagner family and jury has the potential to induce bias in their deliberations. The judge denied the motion for mistrial.

At the end of the second week of deliberations, the jury supervisor asked the court for more jury options, other than murder. The state, defense, and judge agreed to instruct the jury on voluntary manslaughter and reckless homicide. The inherently lesser included offense of murder.

After a short deliberation, the jury marched into the courtroom sometime during the evening. Mrs. Wagner and Sherry Granger were the only two people in the courtroom.

The judge read the verdict. "We the jury find Van Johnson guilty of voluntary manslaughter."

Mrs. Wagner shouted, "Manslaughter?" She could not believe the jury didn't convict me of murder.

A courtroom deputy sheriff consoled her with the statement, "He won't be making that big money anymore." (Class warfare is among the various shades of racism.)

After the verdict, deputies transported me back to the county jail. They placed me in a holding area on the first floor. It was strange not to find any other inmates present. Chavis was the only defense lawyer that came to visit me at the jail following the verdict. He said, "I'm sorry we didn't do anything for you. The prosecution caught us off-guard with how they presented its case." I thought that was strange coming from a guy who repeatedly bragged about being a third-generation lawyer that knew the law game. But wasn't Broderick supposed to give him insight into the various strategies of the prosecutor? Broderick, Nave, and Lawler worked as a team for many years. It gave me the impression that Chavis may have been paid off as well. It was obvious that the trial was a highly staged event. Attorneys Oliver and Broderick did not try to fake their feelings toward me. Black lawyers will sell out their black clients at the drop-of-a-hat, so to speak.

During my sentencing a month later, judge Spencer gave me forty years in prison with ten years suspended. I was shocked! I had a clean record with no prior offenses. That sentence he gave me is the presumptive sentence for murder convictions. The court could have given me probation, or time served – a manslaughter conviction can even be reduced to a misdemeanor! After the sentencing hearing, Lt. Lee George transported me that afternoon to the Indiana Reception and Diagnostics Center in Plainfield, Indiana. Prior to leaving the Anderson area, he drove me by several taverns, barber shops, and homes of people we knew. It gave me a chance to say goodbye to people I had met in that small town. People shook my hand; and some cried. Everyone knew the court system had railroaded me to prison.

Chapter Six

DURING OUR TWO-HOUR TRIP TO THE RDC, LT. GEORGE AND I rehashed the good memories we had together at my home. When we arrived at the RDC administration building, Lt. George lifted me from the back seat of the patrol car. When we entered the administration building, a guard escorted us to a desk in the back where a guard sat. Lt. George handed him a thick yellow packet. He looked at me and said, "Good luck my friend." Then he abruptly walked away. He tried but could not conceal the hurt and sorrow of seeing me enter the prison system.

The RDC is Indiana's central processing facility for newly convicted felons. It is the first phase in a protracted process of institutional depersonalization. Convicts wear the same prison attire; a number replaces your name; everyone eats the same food, at the same time every day. All a person's movements are controlled and monitored in prisons. Everything about you is open for display, which includes your trips to the toilet and shower.

Because my case was high profile and received extensive media coverage, African American correctional officers at the RDC facility expressed their sympathy. Those black officers were shocked to see a black doctor in prison for defending his life at home.

The first thing required of you is a physical and dental examination, blood tests, and complete a Minnesota Multiphasic Personality Inventory (MMPI) -- a 600-word multiple-choice survey. Weeks later, I was taken to the medical clinic to get the results of my medical workup. I met with an Indian doctor. He said that all my blood and urine tests were normal; but according to the analysis of my MMPI survey, I was narcissistic, but had a low antisocial index. "That means you don't have a criminal mind," he said. Since I was from the Chicago area, he would recommend that I be transferred to the Indiana State Prison in Michigan City. It's a short drive from my hometown. Unbeknownst to me, that prison was rumored to be the end-of-the-line and housed the state's most hardened criminals.

923123 was my new name as a prisoner. That number appeared in large font on my photo ID, which is required on all court documents, mail, and commissary orders. Convicts must have their ID cards to use recreational equipment, enter church services, work sites, school classes and libraries.

In September 1992, I arrived at the Indiana State prison in Michigan City, Indiana. The facility resembled a 17th-century fortress with forty-foot-high walls topped off with coils of razor wire. It was the oldest prison in Indiana and once held captured confederate soldiers during the civil war. After the bus entered the back gate guards assisted us into a small building. We had to exchange our RDC uniforms for those worn at that prison. A guard escorted us to the Admission and Orientation building. When I asked the whereabouts of the other prisoners, the guard said the facility was on total lockdown.

We were split up and placed in different sections of the A-and-O building. The units were filthy, noisy, well-lit with numerous cameras. Some convicts were there for disciplinary reasons. Convicts were only allowed out of their cells for showers. There was no outside recreation. The convicts restructured their sleep cycle to stay up all night and sleep all day. At night, the unit got really loud. The convicts threatened each other, traded insults, and lied about their criminal exploits.

The next morning, a guard escorted me to the Hoosier room, a conference room in the administration building. The room had a large table in the center. Nearly everyone at that meeting wore a black suit, white shirt, black tie and shoes. Several officials were from the Department of Corrections central office. The majority were the upper-management team at the Indiana State Prison. There was Mr. B. J. Johnson, a black man who managed an honor dorm, Captain Craig, the lead Captain, and Mr. Penfold, special assistant to the superintendent. Additionally, there were two assistant wardens at ISP and Dr. McLaren, the prison psychiatrist.

Everyone welcomed me. Mr. Penfold, as group spokesman, proceeded straight to their agenda. "We are faced with a dilemma of what to do with you. Should we place you in the general population or in administrative segregation? Our convict population here at the Indiana State prison is seventy-seven percent functionally illiterate. Less than two percent had some college education, and only 0.6% had a bachelor's degree in civilian life." One of the staff characterized them as a bunch of "overgrown children with impulse control problems and dangerous sociopaths." A central office officials said, "Doctor Johnson, you are the only M.D. now serving time in the entire Indiana Department of Corrections."

They all expressed concern for my safety, balanced against the overall security of the institution. They made me aware that my background was extensively reviewed, and all knew that I was a psychiatrist that once practiced at several maximum-security prisons in Illinois.

One assistant warden said, "Because of your knowledge of how hospitals in prisons operate, you'll never have a chance to work in the hospital, or in this administration building at this prison!"

Mr. Penfold issued a warning to me. "We have invested millions of dollars to upgrade our hospital. If you attempt to organize a takeover of our hospital, you will disappear until the courts order your release!"

After he read me about the riot act, Dr. McLaren, the prison psychiatrist, came to my defense. "Dr. Johnson has an excellent reputation in the profession. His criminal conviction was politically motivated in the small town where he set up a practice. I recommend that Dr. Johnson be placed in one of the honor dorms, as opposed to an administrative segregation unit."

Mr. B.J. Johnson added, "The reports on him from the county jail and RDC were negative for any behavior potentially threatening to their security or operations."

After a long palpable silence, I raised my hand, and they allowed me to enter the discussion over my shelter placement. I asked about the nature of an administrative segregation unit, and why was it being discussed as an option for me? An assistant warden responded, "It is a place for convicts with adjustment problems, or that pose a threat to the security and operation of the institution."

The Major entered the discussion. "Dr. Johnson, your educational background and professional work experience gives you the ability to think outside the box."

I responded, "I'm not some big muscular guy that can lift four hundred pounds." The entire staff laughed.

The Major said, "We're prepared for those types. We have something for their asses! The overwhelming majority of convicts resolve their problems by verbal or physical threats. They think in quite simple terms. Heavy thinkers pose the greatest security risks because of their unpredictability and leadership capabilities. Dr. Johnson, your mind is the greatest weapon in this institution.'"

The following morning, a guard escorted me back to the Hoosier conference room. The same individuals were present. But this time, they were more polite and offered me coffee. Mr. BJ Johnson gave a short presentation on prison life. "Convicts have been killed serving time at this prison, many have been injured, and some were raped. Most violent confrontations were not random events and were usually related to drugs, alcohol, gambling, and homosexual activity." He explained that a convict who uses drugs/alcohol on a regular basis can't afford it, and runs up a large debt, which can occur with gambling activities as well. After the debt becomes so high, an interest payment is added to the principal. The person is usually given warnings and a grace period to make some kind of restitution before the violence occurs. It's pay or check-in! To "check-in" means to get transferred into a protective custody unit. This same mechanism happens with homosexual activity, if the homosexual is a prostitute. Another circumstance he cited was having homosexual relations with someone else's punk.

Captain Craig entered the discussion. "Dr. Johnson, you will face a lot of jealousy and envy. I advise you to stay in control of yourself, regardless. The easiest thing to do in prison…is to stay here! There are plenty of weapons in here, and anyone can be killed at any time. We have infiltrated every organization in this prison. There are so many snitches on our payroll in the various gangs, you will never be asked for information on anyone. You can always tell who a snitch is. It is always the convict that is talking about who is snitching! Doctor Johnson, you are not to join a gang or teach those psychopaths anything whatsoever. Do not practice any psychiatry here. You will be closely monitored. Do you get the message?"

I replied, "Yes, I do."

Dr. McLaren, the prison psychiatrist, recommended that I be placed in F-dorm, an honor with older and more mature convicts. Mr. BJ Johnson, the F-dorm supervisor, ended the meeting by wishing me good luck on my direct appeal, to keep a level head, and to stay out of trouble. I was escorted back to the A-and-O unit.

They transferred me to the F-dorm. It was an honor dorm surrounded by a perimeter fence in the northwest corner of the prison. Traffic had to enter through a wooden shack with a metal detector and guard. The outside area had a full basketball court, park benches, and several gardens. After passing through the dorm door, you had to pass through two steel gates to enter the dayroom, where all activities took place. There were pool tables, park benches, weightlifting benches, and a ping-pong table. A floor-to-ceiling chain-link fence separated the dayroom from the showers, washrooms, and cubicles where convicts slept. The dorm was divided into an east and west side. Each side had its own community shower and restroom. There was an elevated guard station positioned in the middle of the dayroom to monitor both sides. Convicts kept their personal items and slept in 9ft. x 6ft. cubicles, surrounded on three sides by a six-foot high brick wall. The cubicles had enough room for two metal cabinets and a twin-size bed. Cigarette smoke had heavily stained the white ceiling tiles and walls.

When I entered the front gate to the west side, a white convict was waiting to assist me to my cubicle. The guard gave me a three-inch mattress, an old dusty burlap blanket, and a combination lock. The 1992 football season had started. Everyone was watching a game on their thirteen-inch color TVs, which required headphones for sound. After sitting my property on the bed, the white convict introduced himself. The worker was a snitch that the officials had briefed about my arrival. The dorm worker invited me to meet a convict named McCormick, another white convict that lived in the back of the dorm. McCormick stopped typing, stood up, and shook my hand. But then he made a quizzical remark, "I'm wondering why the administration would put a psychiatrist among us." Then the rhetorical question, "Might we be subjects in some type of research project?!" I just looked at him and walked away. I knew who not to fuck with.

The next morning, Capt. Craig, two lieutenants, a sergeant, and another guard walked into F-dorm and came directly to my cubicle. The captain addressed me loudly as "Dr. Johnson," then asked if I would complete an emergency commissary form to obtain a TV, coffee pot, radio, headphones, cigarettes, and coffee—food was prohibited on lock-downs. Within several days, I received the items I ordered from the commissary. However, from that day forward, the other convicts and prison staff called me "Doc." Every convict had a nickname in prison.

Guards counted the prison population throughout the day and night. Everyone had to be in their assigned area but did not have to be awake when the lights were off. Convicts had to submit a list of ten people they wanted to call. Their contacts made a monthly payment to the phone company. They monitor and record all calls made from the prison. Relatives and friends were limited to an hour-long visit twice a month.

A few distant relatives and friends placed money in my prison trust fund. Several cousins made monthly visits. One had an expense account with Barnes and Noble. I would order books on her account every month. Mel, my prep school counselor, and a dear friend, paid for my subscriptions to Jet, Ebony, Black Enterprise, Newsweek, Time magazine, New Yorker magazine, and the Chicago Defender newspaper.

I read and wrote during those long days of lockdown. The dorm lights were turned off at 9 p.m. I watched television until morning and then slept until noon. The guards delivered breakfast sacks around 7:00 a.m., when most convicts were asleep. The guards hated the long lock-downs because they had to do the custodial work. The biggest advantage of living in the dorm was more room to move around and an opportunity for a daily shower.

I entered the Indiana State Prison during its fifth month of lock-down. Allegedly precipitated by a series of fatal stabbings at that prison. Every day, I witnessed those tough guys posturing with their profane and threatening language, but it rarely resulted in violence. However, there was one act of violence I will never forget. Early one morning during the lockdown, everyone in the dorm was awakened by lights being turned on. The guards and hospital staff rushed into the dorm to tend to an elderly white convict several cubicles up from me. He was stabbed in the throat with a no. 2 pencil by a young white convict that slept in the adja-cent cubicle to him. The wounded elderly man slowly walked towards the front gate with the shaft of that pencil protruding from his neck. It bobbed with every step as he gasped for air. There was no external hem-orrhaging from the impalement area around the pencil. When several convicts came to his assistance, I warned them not to remove the embed-ded pencil. The old man survived the emergency surgery but succumbed to emphysema months later. He was a reputed Klansman with a reputa-tion for making prison knives (Shanks).

The so-called elite prisoners were housed in the F-dorm. It was only sixty percent occupied and racially balanced. Most whites were skilled tradesmen in civilian life. There were other professionals besides me: a lawyer; a prosecutor; and several engineers. There was an outstanding artist who graduated from the University of California, Berkeley. He received a life sentence for trafficking LSD. Most black convicts in the dorm were high-ranking gang members who were in charge. They called the shots and defused many potentially fatal conflicts and disciplined their soldiers. Both races got along well in the dorm.

The prison environment is like a military barrack. It is a half-step above a shed, garage, or back porch. There are no refinements whatsoever in that environment. During the winter, cold winds off lake Michigan forced us to sleep in our prison-issue clothing. It was my first holiday season in prison. Cable T.V. provided some escape from the harsh reality of that existence. Every television cable channel was available to the convict population. Thanksgiving and Christmas were the only times that convicts received decent meals.

At the end of January 1993, the prison was slowly returning to normal operations. The kitchen, laundry, and industry workers were allowed to go back to their jobs. February 1993, the prison was back to normal operations. The lockdown was over.

Chapter Seven

IN AUGUST 1992, KIRK JOHNSON, MY HALF-BROTHER, NOTED
in a letter that he purchased a home in Allentown, Pennsylvania. He
had enough space to store my property. Kirk contacted Atty. Oliver
and they agreed on a day to meet at the storage facility to pick up my
property. Kirk and Toni, his wife, rented a large truck and drove to
Anderson. They arrived at the storage facility, but Atty. Oliver never
showed up, or answered their phone calls. Kirk had to call Atty. Chavis
in Indianapolis. Chavis drove up to Anderson and let them in the
storage facility. When Kirk completed an inventory of my property, it
became apparent why Atty. Oliver didn't show up: he stole thousands
of dollars' worth of paintings, antiques, statues, jewelry, bookshelves,
the bar and stools, cameras, stereo equipment, and clothing. Kirk
reported the theft to Chavis, who seemed indifferent. He did not give
Kirk an explanation on how Atty. Oliver got on my defense team. Did
the authorities in Anderson threaten and pay off Atty. Chavis too?

In the fall of 1992, Atty. Oliver informed me by mail that the court
was preparing the transcripts of my trial. Judge Spencer had released
funds for David Stone IV to prepare the direct appeal. Several weeks later,
I received a certified letter from the Indiana attorney general. It contained
a questionnaire which sought specific information about the shooting at
my home. It had to be completed and returned before a certain date. I
contacted Chavis, who instructed me to forward the letter to his office
post haste. Chavis sent me a copy of the completed questionnaire he for-
warded to the Indiana medical board and attorney general's office.

In February 1993, the Indiana medical board notified me of the
date of their formal hearing and disposition of my medical license.

In spring 1993, I married Atty. Marguerite Price-Stamps. She was Chairman and CEO of the Universal Human Rights for African People (UHRAP). We had a formal Islamic wedding in the Hoosier room at the Indiana State Prison. Choicia, Verniece and Lois Scaife were my cousins that witnessed the marriage ceremony. In July 1993, Marguerite accompanied Atty. Chavis to the Indiana medical licensing board hearing in Indianapolis. She came to the prison the next day to inform me of what took place at the meeting. "The medical board failed to have enough members for a quorum. One doctor walked out in protest, which left only three members out of the usual fifteen to vote on the disposition of your medical license. Chavis and the lawyer representing the state made a compromise that your license would be revoked, but you would be allowed to reapply later if you met the medical standards required at that time."

Cosmetically, the medical board spared me "Permanent Suspension," the most severe sanction a doctor can face. However, I was under no illusion that my life in medicine was over.

In February 1993, Atty. David Stone IV notified me that he had received the twenty-four volumes of court transcripts. It would take time to thoroughly review those records. I never understood why Judge Fred Spencer paid thousands of dollars for an elite legal research firm to ghost-write my direct appeal. Atty. Oliver was the appellate counsel on record and would get credit for the successful appeal.

I was the only convict in f-dorm with no work assignment. The administration placed me on "medical idle" status because of my hypertension. They were allowing me to slowly adapt to the normal operating routines of prison life. While the other prisoners were at work, there was only me and a dorm worker named Long, in that supermarket size building. He was the top pool shark in the prison. I watched him wipe out challengers in minutes. After finishing his duties, he kicked my ass daily on that pool table. Since I had nothing to do, I practiced shooting pool while others were at work. It took me several years, but my skills dramatically improved. One day, I finally beat the expert. It elevated my status among other convicts. A lot of them admired my ability to adapt to their world.

My only chance of interacting with other convicts in the general population was during chow lines at breakfast, lunch, or dinner. The largest exposure to the convict population was during the lunch period. After their meal, convicts hung out under a row of trees on what they called main street. Some of the convicts creeped into other housing units to suck a dick, fuck a punk, get fucked, drink hooch, smoke dope, or gamble. After several hours, guards would form a line and slowly walk down the main street as a signal that lunch was over, and to clear the street.

The old chow hall once showed movies, evidenced by its downward slanted floor. A guard sat in the former viewing booth holding a long rifle at chow time. Convicts ate on park benches. Black convicts were served in a line to the left, whites on the right side as they entered the chow hall.

I met the guy that organized the prison's Lifer organization. I found out that eighty-five percent of convicts at ISP are serving life sentences. Some of the convicts called me "short timer" because of my short sentence. I viewed that place as a mobile cemetery because many convicts would eventually die inside those prison walls. Unless their families claimed the bodies, when convicts died, their bodies were interred in a prison graveyard adjacent to the prison. Their graves were marked with a wooden cross bearing their D.O.C. number.

Monday through Friday, outside recreation was from 4.30 p.m. to 8.30 p.m. Saturdays and Sundays, it was 8.00 a.m. to 12:00 p.m. All cell houses and dorms went to recreation simultaneously. The recreation yard had a half-mile oval-shaped jogging track, basketball court, baseball field with bleachers, and an area for pitching horseshoes. Inside the fieldhouse was a basketball court, free weights and benches, pool tables, and video games. There was a room where you could check out equipment and obtain bags of ice.

The older convicts were more mature with more refined social skills to manage skirmishes without resorting to physical violence. My routine started with a two-mile power walk. Then I lifted weights with some of the youngsters, who helped me develop proper techniques. The physical regiment kept me healthy to deal with the stress. This was the lowest-low point in my life. But it unveiled a compelling truth: as a Black man, I had no family or friends…just true enemies! Not one member of my so-called "saved-and-sanctified" family attended the trial. They did not care what happened, or why. But even stranger, not one representative from a black media outlet covered my trial.

I was surprised when Vera Dupree sent me a letter. It noted the name of an acquaintance in that prison. He was a native of Anderson who was going to be released from that prison soon. One evening at recreation, I noticed a well-built light-skinned man with dreadlocks staring at me as I left the recreation building. We looked at each other with curiosity. I walked up to him and asked if we had a mutual friend. He smiled and introduced himself as Murphy, and said, "Vera told me about your story and to watch your back." We routinely jogged together at the beginning of the recreation period. Murphy mentioned that his conviction took place in the same circuit court system in Anderson. He disclosed some information that only someone well acquainted with my case would know. One evening during our workout, Murphy looked me in the eye and said, "I know for a fact that you were framed and railroaded into prison!" When I asked him to prove it, he reacted with a shit-eating grin on his face.

Murphy was quiet, circumspect, and had the focused stare of a scholar. He gave me a brief history of everyone that we encountered in the recreation yard. Murphy was not gang-affiliated, but he disclosed the structured interactions within large group settings. The church services and dining hall were used as examples. Rarely did we see a random act of violence during recreation periods. A code of conduct existed within-and-between the gangs. If two individuals had a serious dispute, they would go to the restroom and duke it out for a few rounds. The combatants were prohibited from using weapons during those brawls. If a combatant was knocked down, or knocked out, they stopped the fight. After the battle, the combatants would exit the restroom as if nothing happened. A major confrontation between rival gangs would lead to a large casualty and result in an immediate lockdown, cessation of visits, phone calls, hot meals, daily showers, commissary, and stop the flow of illicit drugs and money. Many convicts had street survival skills but lacked any formal education.

In August 1994, one evening after recreation, Murphy and I were walking down main street and encountered a short, red-headed, freckle-faced white man. Murphy asked if we had met. Murphy introduced him as 'Red.' He introduced me as 'Doc.' Red said his real name was James Ericksen. Red asked me, "Are you, Dr. Van Johnson the psychiatrist?" I said yes. Ericksen displayed a sarcastic smile and asked, "Are you now practicing psychiatry at this prison?"

I responded, "I'm a prisoner like you and everyone else here."

Ericksen appeared puzzled and said, "So, they actually convicted you of that shooting?" Ericksen then said, "I committed many burglaries with that man you killed." He continued, "As a matter of fact, he burglarized your medical office searching for drugs. People are aware that psychiatrists keep a lot of samples in their office." He was correct in that my office was burglarized in March of 1990. The police did not make a report and it was not noted in the newspapers.

When I confirmed the office burglary, Ericksen talked at length about James Wagner's criminal lifestyle. "He worked the third-shift at a general motor's plant. In the early 1970s, we committed hundreds of burglaries together in Madison County. He was a very heavy drinker, drug user, and a violent man that committed armed robberies. In April 1990, Wagner had told me he had been checking out a young black doctor from Chicago, who recently opened a practice in Anderson. He said the doctor lived in the Cross Lakes luxury apartment complex. Since his children had a paper route in that area, he had an excuse to be over there. Wagner said that when you were at the office, he had checked out the contents of your apartment numerous times. He had followed you to-and-from work and studied your routine. Wagner also knew the management at your apartment complex. He would often bring up your name to elicit conversation about your lifestyle. The management at the housing complex was pissed that you had two white female housekeepers and an all-white office staff. Wagner said he was going to break into the home, and if you're there, kill you!'"

James Ericksen said that the last time he had met with Wagner was in April 1990. He recalled people telling him that Wagner was killed but eventually saw it in the media. It shocked him to learn that Wagner was killed by a black Doctor from Chicago at the Crosslake apartments complex. Ericksen prepared a sworn statement with dates and addresses of unsolved burglaries that he and Wagner had committed in the Anderson area and sent it to Judge Fred Spencer. He knew that Spencer was the presiding judge in my case. (Judge Spencer at no time, mentioned receiving that affidavit From Mr. Ericksen. Did he "Hoodwink" the prosecutor and my defense team?)

Ericksen asked if I knew a police detective named Rodney Cummings. On my face sheet, Cummings was listed as an investigator in the case. Ericksen said that Cummings had recently been elected as the Madison County prosecutor, the first Felon in U.S. history to be elected a prosecutor. "Cummings served time for a burglary conviction at the Pendleton Reformatory and had participated in burglaries with me and Wagner years ago. He received a pardon, which allowed him to become an Anderson police officer," he said.

The court, state, or defense team never mentioned receiving Ericksen's affidavit. Did some clerk or secretary at the courthouse destroy that document? Ericksen's testimony at trial would've provided the corroborating statement that Spencer claimed he needed to believe James Wagner had attacked me. The white community simply wanted revenge! If Spencer had made that affidavit known, the lynch mob would've had him removed from the bench or assassinated him.

Mrs. Jan Wagner used her media connections to whitewash her husband's character: They presented him as the all-American white guy. They presented me as your typical savage nigger.

Mr. Ericksen never sought any financial gain in exchange for exposing Wagner's criminal past. I believe providing me with that information gave Ericksen a chance to clear his conscience on the matter. Ironically, when I asked if he needed any money, Ericksen reacted with disgust,

"Why would I accept your money when I could've just not told you a damn thing?" He walked away and never spoke to me again. I felt embarrassed and regretted coming to him that way. I prayed that Ericksen would forgive me for that act of desperation.

In June 1995, I was returning from the chow hall after lunch, to play some pinochle in the dorm. As I was walking down main street, convicts from other shelters were on their way to the chow hall. The main street was suddenly crowded with convicts going in the opposite direction to me. In prison, you quickly learn to mind your business and avoid staring at people during movements, i.e. keep one's gaze straight forward when approaching a crowd. On that day, Ericksen emerged from the approaching crowd and handed me a legal-size manila envelope. I went straight to my cubicle and hastily opened the envelope. Mr. James H. Erickson had prepared an affidavit that was signed and dated June 4, 1995.

I felt like a burden was lifted off my soul. I immediately sent the original to judge Spencer, and copies to every defense attorney, private investigator, friends, and family.

Dr. Robert Lackey had never written to me since my incarceration. But after I sent him a copy of Ericksen's affidavit, he responded by writing me a letter that ended with, "All doubts have been removed!" I'm sure he shared that document with our frat brothers in Indianapolis.

James Ericksen's original affidavit that was sent to Judge Spencer, was most likely hidden or destroyed. As a result, Ericksen's affidavit had no impact on this trial.

AFFIDAVIT OF JAMES H. ERIKSEN

Having first been duly sworn and upon his oath, states as follows:

1. I have personal knowledge of the events subject to this affidavit.

2. I have known one James Waggner since 1977 when I was running around with Lyndal Glenn.

3. We were doing residential and business burglaries together.

4. I used to trade drugs with James Waggner.

5. I used to sell cocaine, crack and Valium to James Waggner.

6. James Waggner would threaten to stick up drugstores or drug dealers when he couldn't buy drugs.

7. At one time James Waggner owned several handguns which he wanted to trade for cocaine.

8. At one time I met him at General Motors, his employer, and traded with him.

9. On many occasions I would drive with him to case the homes of influential persons such as lawyers, judges and doctors because he wanted to break into them and tear up everything inside them and hurt or kill whoever was there.

10. James Waggner's drinking and drug use changed his attitude towards people with power and money and wanted to rob and hurt them.

11. During the month of April, 1990 I saw James Waggner

DR. VAN JOHNSON, M.D.

while I was on Work Release and he told me that he was checking out this black doctor's house that he wanted to burglarize so that he could get some money and drugs.

12. James Waggner also told me that it would not matter because the police would think that a black man broke into the home anyway.

13. The next time I heard about James Waggner was when I got word that he had been shot and killed.

14. After hearing about the I wrote a letter to Judge Spencer telling him of the events and things that James Waggner had done leading up to the incident in which he was shot.

I affirm under the penalties for perjury that the above representations are true to the best of my knowledge and further the affiant sayeth not.

Dated   June 4, 1995

James H. Eriksen # 860138
Indiana State Prison
P. O. Box 41
Michigan City, IN 46361-0041

118

Chapter Eight

IN **SPRING** **1994, I**NDIANA**'**S **APPELLATE** **COURT** **AFFIRMED** the conviction. Atty. David Stone IV notified me that he was preparing a Petition to Transfer to have the appellate court decision reviewed by the Indiana Supreme Court. It is very rare for the state's highest court to review an appellate court decision. Atty. Stone sent me a copy of the petition and the legal brief. He exhaustively argued two issues:1) The trial court abused its discretion in allowing testimony about the uncharged misconduct in the fire-extinguisher incident at my home. 2) the trial court erred in not allowing jury instructions on self-defense.

In February 1995, the Indiana supreme court granted permission to transfer. It meant that they would review the appellate court's ruling. They ordered all lower courts to forward any records of the case to the supreme court. A lawyer serving time at the prison opined, "If the Supreme court granted permission to transfer, there was an obvious serious flaw on the face of the record, too pervasive to be ruled a harmless error. The conviction has a seventy percent chance of being overturned."

On September 25, 1995, I began an uneventful day at my job in the prison tag shop making license plates. My shift ended at 2 p.m. that day. I went back to the dorm to play pinochle with another convict named Ray. We were playing at a table in the day room when Boo Sawyer, a high-ranking gang member, walked up and stood next to me at the table. Boo asked, "Hey Doc, when was the last time you heard from your lawyers?" I ignored the question and resumed my card game. Boo walked to the back of the dorm. I noticed a small crowd of high-ranking gang members slowly walking back-and-forth near the back of the dorm. Boo huddled with them along the back wall. Then he returned to my card table and said, "Doc, put those damn cards down and follow me!" I was very apprehensive because everyone in that crowd was silent. That is usually a prelude to violence in prison. I wondered why that group stared at me as I approached them. When we reached the last cubicle, Boo pointed to an Indianapolis Star newspaper lying on a bed in someone's cubicle. He told me to sit down and read it. The newspaper was dated September 25, 1995. The headline and article on page two were written by Mike Smith of the Associated Press. "Supreme Court Overturns Psychiatrist's Manslaughter Conviction." The article noted that the Indiana Supreme court reversed my conviction based on testimony about a prior uncharged incident, which should not have been allowed. The jury had convicted me of voluntary manslaughter in the 1990 slaying of James Wagner: my newspaper carrier's father. The jury found me innocent of murder but guilty of the much lesser offense of manslaughter. I was sentenced to forty years. "Johnson claimed the shooting was accidental and told police that Wagner rushed him after darting from window-to-window of his apartment. Neighbors and Wagner's family testified that Wagner was only collecting for newspaper delivery. Johnson's blood-alcohol content tested at .22 percent five hours after the shooting. Drunkenness in Indiana is a blood alcohol level of .10 percent," cited Mike Smith. The article failed to note that the shooting occurred around 9 p.m. on a Sunday night. The state medical examiner failed to disclose Wagner's toxicology profile. I was not driving a car when this incident occurred. At trial, no one presented proof that I owed a newspaper debt.

I was in a state of shock after reading that article—dazed and confused! After regaining my scruples, I thanked Boo Sawyer. When I stood up, the group lined up then shook my hand and congratulated me. The last to shake my hand was a high-ranking Vice Lord who spoke for the group. "Doc, you stick out like a sore thumb in this place. We are criminals and know who belongs here. You are not a criminal and don't belong in this place. We knew it from the first day you arrived. Have you ever wondered why no one ever stole your property, attacked, or extorted you? We told our soldiers and the white gangs that you were not to be fucked with. We're glad to see a black man among us that received a favorable ruling in this racist court system." One of the guys started pouring hooch (wine) from a large five-gallon bag into sport cups. They toasted me. The guards stayed at their posts.

I immediately called Mel and told her the Indiana Supreme court overturned my conviction. She made a three-way call to Atty. David Stone's office. He answered the phone and said oral arguments before the high court started at 7 a.m. that morning. All nine judges ruled in my favor. "They can't recharge you with murder, but you could be recharged with manslaughter, which involves a different charging instrument," he said.

When I spoke with Chavis, he said that my conviction was reversed on a trial error and that they were going to retry the case.

The following day, an asst. superintendent, the Major, Capt. Craig, a lieutenant, and several sergeants entered F dorm. They signed in and had a brief conversation with the officer in charge (OIC). I was battling Mr. Long on the pool table and paid them no attention. Captain Craig came over to briefly watch the game. Then he interrupted it to congratulate me on the victory in the Supreme court. We shook hands. He wished me good luck in the future. The other officials then came over and expressed their kudos.

I received an official copy of the opinion from Atty. Oliver several months later. The conviction was reversed because the trial court abused its discretion in allowing the jury to hear evidence of uncharged misconduct in violation of trial rule 404B. The prejudicial evidence was allowed for the purpose of proving that I had a criminal character. The supreme court reaffirmed the doctrine. "A person's character" cannot be put on trial.

In November 1995, I filed a formal complaint against Atty. Oliver with the Indiana supreme court disciplinary commission for the theft of my private property. The commission confirmed the receipt of that complaint and that they would investigate the matter.

I worked in the prison tag shop repairing micro-switches, which resembles eight-track tapes. They power the circuits of huge embossers that press numbers and letters on metal templates. In that prison, all the license plates for cars, motorcycles and Dog tags were created for the entire state of Indiana. They produced an average of 75,000 license plates per day. It was here in this building where I gained firsthand experience of illiteracy within the convict population: A black convict in his twenties had a job as a janitor, but he was going to be released on parole soon. During fifteen-minute smoke breaks, workers huddled in groups, drank coffee, and smoked cigarettes. This young janitor had a newspaper opened in his hand when he addressed the crowd. "Does anyone know if Green Bay, Wisconsin is located in South Bend, Indiana?" Everybody first looked at him, and then each other in disbelief. No one said a thing. Most workers acted like they did not hear a thing. I crept into the restroom area and fell on the floor with a gut-wrenching laugh, a laugh I had not had in a long time.

Christmas evening 1995, they allowed the convicts to stay in the day room until midnight. It was one of the few times they allowed me to run a poker game. Here I was at the head of the poker table, sipping Canadian club whiskey from a sports cup. In a lot of ways, prison is no different from society: with money, you could purchase drugs, alcohol, cell phones, special food, and sex from female prison guards. The only thing you could not do is drive a car upon the grounds of the facility. Life in the honor dorm was a little like the prison scene in the movie *Goodfellas*.

On January 15, 1996, I was dressed in a sweat suit ready for outdoor recreation. When they opened the dorm gate to release the crowd for recreation, six guards led by a Sargeant were coming towards the checkpoint. The Sargent pointed and called my name. They surrounded me and escorted me to the guard hall. The Sargent told me there was a Madison County sheriff deputy waiting to transport me back to Anderson to be recharged. "Don't worry, your belongings will be secured and shipped to the county jail," he said.

When I arrived at the Madison County detention center, they placed me with two other men in a special cellblock segregated from all the others in the jail. We were not allowed recreation, work assignments, or commissary. They had instituted a new phone system in the jail: inmates had to get prepaid debit cards to make phone calls. I was effectively cut off from the outside world because prison officials did not allow me to take my phone books; the money from my prison trust fund was never transferred to me at the jail.

On January 22, 1996, they held my arraignment in Judge Spencer's courtroom. Atty. Rodney Cummings was the new Madison County prosecutor. I remembered what Ericksen disclosed about him. Atty. Montague Oliver was my public defender. The courtroom was empty of spectators. Atty. Cummings read the charging instrument. "Van Johnson is being charged with Voluntary manslaughter. He knowingly killed Mr. James Wagner under 'Sudden Heat.'" Cummings requested the court not to issue a bond. Judge Spencer replied, "Mr. Cummings, this is not a murder case anymore. I will set the bond at $35,000.00 cash only. He will not be allowed to leave the county if the Bond is posted." Atty. Cummings added, "his chances of employment in this county would be next-to-none." Atty. Oliver moved to release me on my own recognizance. Spencer denied that motion.

Follow this carefully. I was originally charged with murder, acquitted at trial, but convicted of voluntary manslaughter. The Indiana Supreme Court reversed that manslaughter conviction. Voluntary manslaughter is an inherently lesser included offense of murder. They share the same elements of intentionally or knowingly killing another human being. However, "sudden heat" mitigates murder to manslaughter. If voluntary manslaughter is charged as a stand-alone offense, the state must prove the elements of murder, but now must prove "Sudden heat" beyond a reasonable doubt.

I asked Atty. Oliver to move the court for a dismissal on the grounds that I was being placed in double jeopardy. An acquittal for murder usually bars prosecution for the lesser included offense of voluntary manslaughter "When the manslaughter is overturned on appeal." The plea of double jeopardy must be made at arraignment, or before a jury is impaneled and sworn in. When Oliver refused my request, I moved the court for a change of counsel. "Your honor, I filed a formal complaint against Atty. Oliver with the supreme court disciplinary commission. As you are probably aware, I never wanted him on my defense team."

Oliver countered, "Judge, I move for leave to withdraw from this case. I don't care if he goes back to prison."

Atty. Cummings stated, "His request for a change of counsel should be denied. It would open the door for other defendants who didn't like their attorney to simply file a complaint with that commission."

Judge Spencer added, "The motions for change of counsel and 'leave to withdraw' are denied. You two are going to work together, regardless."

I moved the court to admit Mr. James H. Eriksen's sworn statement into the record as newly discovered evidence. Atty. Cummings objected, "Anyone in prison could've made up that story." Judge Spencer read the sworn statement out loud and mentioned when Lyndal Glenn was killed in a home invasion—a person Ericksen noted in the affidavit. Spencer responded to Cummings' objection, "I hear what you are saying, but that didn't occur in this case. I know Mr. Ericksen, he had a case in my court. I will allow this sworn statement into the court record."

On March 29, 1996, Atty. Oliver filed the motion, ***"Notice of Indigence and request for expenses for payment of necessary Expenses and Costs for the defense of the defendant."*** He requested $600.00 to purchase me a suit for the second trial. Oliver noted that I was estranged from my family and had no money. He noted that I objected and did not desire to appear in jail clothes at trial, which raised this issue to the level of fundamental due process: A defendant can appear at trial in jail clothes if he chooses. But if he "objects" to being tried in jail clothes, it's a violation of his fundamental right to due process and a fair trial. Estelle v. Williams, 425 U.S. 501 (1976), is the controlling case law on this issue.

On April 1, 1996, the court held the only pre-trial conference. It was about Oliver's motion for expenses. Spencer declared that the six-hundred dollars requested for clothing would not be allowed. Oliver responded, "Mr. Johnson is estranged from his family and has no money. Judge, I would accept a lesser amount, or whatever the court would allow. How about I just get him a pair of pants, two shirts, and a jacket?"

Atty. Cummings answered, "It is absurd to purchase any clothing for him. We do not do it for other defendants."

Judge Spencer refused Oliver's compromise and denied the motion. "I won't release any funds for clothing!" There is no standard that governs the amount of money a court may allow for clothing. Spencer acknowledged the formal objection to being tried in jail clothes. "It would be against the law to allow him in court at trial[sic] in those blue jail clothes. I am obligated to make sure that doesn't happen. If he does not have proper attire by 5-29-1996, I will convene a special hearing to resolve this issue."

Oliver told Spencer, "I request leave to withdraw, and don't care about this upcoming trial." Oliver never made a visit during my six-month pre-trial detention at the county jail, and never accepted a collect call from the jail. There was no emergency court hearing prior to the May 29, 1996, deadline.

The six-month pretrial detention was pure hell for me in that county jail. I slept under a thin, filthy, burlap blanket, and a two-inch plastic mattress. The cell block was intentionally kept at a low temperature. The sink in my cell had a rusted spout that constantly dribbled. The toilet was lined with a permanent shit stain. Dead insects discarded plastic utensils and discarded soiled underwear littered the shower. I asked a guard why they allowed these types of conditions to exist in the jail. "Hopefully, it would discourage people from coming to jail." Every night, the guards conducted Gestapo-like shakedowns in every cell.

On June 4, 1996, my trial was scheduled to commence. However, when sheriff's deputies didn't transport me that morning, I called Oliver's office. He accepted my call and said the trial was postponed until June 17, 1996. He assured me that I would have appropriate clothing for the trial. When I asked why they did not hold a court hearing on the issue, Oliver hung up.

The morning of June 7, 1996, two deputies entered my cell and ordered me to get dressed. When I asked where they were taking me, I heard the familiar voice of a dispatcher named Barbara over their radios. She said, "No use fighting, they're going to find you guilty anyway." They allowed me to brush my teeth. I was taken away in dirty, wrinkled blue jailhouse clothing and shower shoes. After we arrived at the courthouse,

I sat on a bench in the foyer of Spencer's second-floor office. He came out with a judicial robe over his forearm and ordered the deputies to remove my handcuffs and leg shackles. Atty. Oliver arrived minutes later. He and spencer had a conversation. Spencer put on his robe and left through a different door. Oliver then informed me that my trial was about to start. He was disheveled with bloodshot eyes, spittle in the corners of his mouth and reeked of alcohol.

When deputies escorted me into the courtroom, the jury box was already filled with the venire jury. The other potential jurors sat in the empty auditorium, which was unusual for such a high-profile case like mine. I found out from Ollie Henderson Dixon, Anderson's only Black alderman, and city council president, why no one attended my second trial. "Every Black minister, politician, nightclub owner, and factory worker had planned to attend your trial. Black folks wanted to see what lie they were going to spin this time. However, a week before the trial, the Anderson Herald Bulletin published a notice that the trial had been postponed, and they would publish well in advance of the new trial date. A month later, they published that the jury convicted you of manslaughter at the second trial. You must serve the ten years suspended on the original sentence." That is the subterfuge that black people deal with daily. Now, Black people see how the media is complicit in their destruction. They gave James Wagner an alibi by lying that he came to my home to collect anewspaper debt.

When Spencer brought the court to the session, he asked Oliver if the defense had anything to say. Oliver asked me to stand up and described my attire as that worn by inmates at the county jail. Spencer asked, "Whose fault, was it?"

Atty. Oliver answered, "It was my understanding that Mr. Johnson's family was going to provide his clothing for trial, but they haven't brought them." I stood up and called that black mf a liar. I explained that my family did not make any arrangements to provide any clothing for the trial. After I rebutted Oliver's false allegation, I moved the court for a Mistrial. Spencer asked me to explain why. I brought up the declaration he made at the pre-trial conference. "Judge, you said it would be against the law for me to be allowed into the courtroom wearing jail clothes at trial."

He denied my motion for mistrial, "We're going ahead with this trial regardless." When I motioned to have the entire jury pool dismissed and replaced, Spencer told me to sit down and shut up.

Judge Spencer asked Oliver, "Would you like a fifteen-minute recess to take Dr. Johnson to goodwill and purchase him a one-dollar shirt?" Oliver remained silent. Spencer continued, "This trial will proceed as planned. Now bring in the jury!" He falsified the events of the trial proceeding. The jury was already present when the sheriff's deputies brought me into the courtroom.

At Voir dire, the state struck the only potential negro juror because she had a relative with a past criminal case in the Madison circuit court. Oliver struck the only white female on the panel because her father was a doctor at St. John's hospital. Both potential female jurors were replaced with elderly white men. The final jury panel consisted of twelve elderly white men.

During Voir dire, Atty. Oliver's drunken behavior was an embarrassment. While questioning the jurors up close, he showered them with spittle. They wiped their red faces in disbelief. People in the audience snickered and some laughed aloud. Spencer had to gavel the court back to order. It looked like a skit from the Three Stooges.

Atty. Oliver questioned a juror named Mr. C.P. "The fact that they brought Mr. Johnson in here and charged him with a crime, does that mean anything to you?

The juror said, "It implies he's guilty…he's in jail attire!" Judge Spencer did not issue any remedial instructions to the jury following his prejudicial comment.

Atty. Puckett, an assistant prosecutor that was assigned to litigate the case against me. Cummings had to recuse himself because he was a police investigator on my case. Prior to presenting his opening statement, he and Oliver were whispering while transferring the records to different folders.

Spencer requested the transcript of the police investigator that previously testified that Wagner's blood was not tested for drugs or alcohol. Spencer read aloud, "So the late Mr. Wagner's blood was negative for drugs or alcohol." This crooked Judge was altering facts already on the record. I vehemently denied his claim, "That is not true. The investigator testified that they only tested Wagner's urine. Please let me inspect Wagner's blood toxicology report?"

Spencer angrily replied, "I do not have to prove anything to you! If you say one more thing in this court, I will hold you in contempt."

When the court was brought to the session, Atty. Puckett presented the charging instrument. "Van Johnson is charged by information with the crime of voluntary Manslaughter. He knowingly killed James Wagner while acting under sudden heat." The court played my recorded statement to the police on the night of the shooting. But the jury was never shown the crime scene videotapes and crime scene photos! For clarity and brevity, only the salient features of the states and defense's case-in-chief will be noted. Atty. Puckett presented the state's case-in-chief. "The elements of this charge are that he knowingly or intentionally killed. It's not charged as an accident, reckless, or anything else. He knew what he was doing. It could not have been an accident. How much more reckless can you be than to meet somebody at your front door with a shotgun aimed at them, the safety off, and ready to fire? Why? Because Wagner peeked into his window? Mr. Johnson was guilty of violating Indiana Criminal code 35-47-4-3 (criminal recklessness, a misdemeanor) when he pointed that gun at Mr. Wagner."

Atty. Oliver objected, "He was never charged with that offense," and then moved for a mistrial. His motion was denied. In a homicide trial, no mention or consideration should be given to a lesser non-homicide offense. Puckett did not illustrate or mention one example of "Sudden Heat." Atty. Oliver presented the defense case-in-chief. "What happened on the night of June 10, 1990, at Mr. Johnson's home was a tragic accident. As you noticed on the recording of his statement to the police, his speech was slurred and interrupted by numerous hiccups. He did not know Mr. Wagner and could not have knowingly killed him."

Atty. Chavis entered the courtroom. Oliver asked the court to swear him in as a witness for the defense. Puckett objected, "Atty. Chavis previously served on Mr. Johnson's defense team. Now he is going to testify as a witness in the same case. I am worried about the sanctity of client-attorney confidentiality." The Judge admonished both sides on the possible perils of such a maneuver but allowed Chavis to take the witness stand. Atty. Oliver asked, "How did you and Dr. Johnson become acquainted?"

Atty. Chavis responded, "Dr. Johnson retained me after St. John's hospital terminated his contract." Atty. Puckett objected to any elaboration about that matter with the hospital. The Judge agreed and sustained his objection.

Atty. Oliver asked, "At some point, did that professional relationship become personal?"

Atty. Chavis answered, "Yes. I made numerous visits to Dr. Johnson's medical office and his home. I met Sonja, his fiancée from Chicago. She prepared dinner for us at his home. Dr. Johnson and Sonja attended my son's reception after his graduation from law school." Attorney Puckett waived cross-examination. (Because I called Chavis prior to notifying police after the shooting, there was speculation that we had planned Wagner's murder.) I believe Chavis was put on the witness stand to nullify those rumors and clear his reputation. Why would a wealthy Black attorney conspire with a black psychiatrist to kill a white factory worker that neither of them knew?

The few witnesses who took the stand during the second trial presented no new facts in the case. Their testimonies did not differ from the ones they gave at the previous trial.

The state or defense did not discuss or show any objective evidence. The jury was not shown any pictorial evidence or crime scene videotape. The police and prosecutor's office knew they had used tainted evidence to convict me. So, the evidence was destroyed after the first trial, because no one expected that conviction to be overturned. The judge later admitted that the photographic evidence and crime scene videotape had disappeared.

Atty. Puckett presented the state's closing argument. "The state has proved the elements of the crime. Mr. Johnson intentionally and knowingly killed James Wagner. His conduct on the night of the shooting was pervasively reckless, however, I am not arguing reckless or any other lesser offense. He knowingly killed Mr. Wagner. It was not an accident." (Sudden Heat beyond a reasonable doubt was never illustrated or mentioned.)

Attorney Oliver's closing argument was next. "Mr. Wagner's death was a tragic accident. The state did not prove that Mr. Johnson knowingly killed Mr. Wagner, while under sudden heat. As a matter of fact, the state never illustrated any evidence of sudden heat; and introduced recklessness into its case-in-chief and closing argument. Mr. Johnson stated he did not mean to kill Mr. Wagner. He is a medical doctor that attended Harvard university, something I could never accomplish." Then rested his case.

Judge Spencer held a sidebar to request jury instructions that both sides wanted presented to jurors. Puckett only requested instructions on voluntary manslaughter. Oliver requested instructions on accident, lack of intent, voluntary intoxication, and 'the state failed to prove its burden.' Spencer agreed only to give jury instructions on Voluntary Manslaughter, Accident, and Voluntary Intoxication. Ironically, he failed to properly instruct the jury on all matters of law prior to giving those instructions.

Once the instructions were given to the jury, Judge Spencer 'Sua Sponte' announced that the jury would be given instructions on self-defense. Atty. Oliver vehemently objected. "Your honor, there was no evidence of self-defense in this case!" Oliver was correct. The new evidence in this case was never subpoenaed to testify at trial. The jury weighs all evidence. A judge may Sua sponte issue instructions on self-defense if there is some evidence to support it, or if the theory of the defense is inconsistent. However, the defense consistently stated the shooting was a tragic accident. Self-defense and accident are affirmative but inconsistent defenses when presented in the same case. When the court instructs the jury on a defensive issue, it becomes law applicable to the case. But the court can never Sua sponte issue an instruction on self-defense over the objection of the defense." Mullaney v. Wilbur, 421 U.S. 684, 704, 95 S. Ct. 1881, 1892 (1975). Matthew v. The United States (1988) 485 U.S. 58, 63-64.)

Neither the state nor the defense requested a jury instruction on self-defense. When Judge Spencer instructed the jury on self-defense over the objection of defense counsel, he abused his discretion and violated my fundamental right to due process and a fair trial. That jury instruction confused and misled the jury as to a correct understanding of the law, and it forced them to resolve an issue that did not exist.

Oliver displayed ineffective assistance of counsel by failing to subpoena Mr. James Ericksen to testify at trial. The court allowed his affidavit into the record of proceedings as new evidence. This violated my right to a complete defense under the fifth, sixth, and fourteenth Amendments to the U.S. constitution.

Judge Spencer failed to instruct the jury on a profoundly serious evidentiary dispute: Did I have a "reckless" or "knowing" state of mind when Wagner was shot? It was the state that injected "recklessness" into their case-in-chief and closing argument. Reckless homicide is an inherently lesser offense of voluntary manslaughter. The only distinguishing feature between the two offenses is the lesser culpability required to establish reckless homicide.

The court erred when it failed to issue Sua sponte jury instructions on the lesser offense of Reckless Homicide: the jury was left with an all-or-nothing choice. The state cannot draft information that forecloses an instruction on an inherently lesser-included offense. **Aeschliman v. State (1992), Ind, 589 N.E. 2D 1160, 1161.** This was a fundamental error that violated my right to due process and a fair trial.

Puckett said in the closing argument, "The state has proved the elements," but he failed to illustrate sudden heat beyond a reasonable doubt, which is mandatory if voluntary manslaughter is charged as a stand-alone offense. That failure violated my protection against double jeopardy under the Fifth Amendment.

The elderly all-white male jury took only ten minutes to reach a guilty verdict. Spencer changed the original sentence of forty years with ten suspended to me having to serve the entire forty-year sentence, "There's no new aggravating circumstance, I just want you to do this time," he said. A murder conviction in Indiana usually carries a presumptive sentence of forty years. Spencer told me to write to the court if I wanted the conviction appealed.

The following are the fundamental errors that violated my right to due process and a fair second trial: 1) The trial court compelled me to stand trial in jail clothes. 2) Atty. Oliver failed to present newly discovered evidence at trial. 3) the state failed to illustrate "Sudden Heat" beyond a reasonable doubt, thus subjecting me to Double Jeopardy in violation of the Fifth Amendment. 4)The trial court abused its discretion by issuing Sua sponte jury instructions on self-defense over defense objection. 5)The trial court failed to Sua sponte issue jury instructions on Reckless Homicide.

The fundamental errors must be raised on direct appeal or be considered waived. The waiver forecloses post-conviction relief because the state post-conviction court does not allow litigation of fundamental errors.

Chapter Nine

THEY TRANSFERRED ME TO THE PENDLETON REFORMATORY, which surprised me because I told the Department of Corrections officials that my relatives worked there. Also, I had signed a contract to chair their department of psychiatry. Convicts are rarely taken to prisons where their relatives are employed. I had a hunch that something far more sinister was at work.

After going to the orientation unit, the staff refused my repeated request for an indigent hygiene kit. (Officials at the Indiana State Prison never transferred my personal property or money to the county jail.) As a result, I went days without a toothbrush, soap, or shampoo. My shit-smelling breath and funky body odor led other convicts to view me as a social outcast. I received horrible insults about my poor hygiene. But things changed when the convicts found out that the prison staff had refused to get my property, trust fund account, and denied my repeated requests for an indigent kit. The convicts started purchasing hygiene products on my behalf.

I went to the dental office to schedule an appointment. The guard on duty lived in Anderson. He told me that my friend Dr. Robert Lackey had passed away. Dr. Eugene Roach was now the prison's chair of psychiatry. I wondered if Dr. Roach was forced to resign as medical director from the Anderson Center. I put in a request to the psych department but never received an appointment. Roach thought that I was going to kill him.

I remembered when members of the Scaife family visited me at the county jail. I heard that some of them held various positions here at the Reformatory. Scaife' was on the name tag of the officer that led our cellhouse to breakfast every morning. One morning, I asked Ofc. Wayne Scaife if we were related. He said our fathers were first cousins and their family was aware of my circumstance.

Every morning during breakfast we caught up on family history. However, in prison there is a convict code—don't talk or be friendly with guards. One morning, a convict asked why I conversed with Officer Scaife every morning. To avoid the "snitch" label, I revealed that Officer Scaife and I were cousins. He asked if I could get Wayne to bring some contraband into the prison. I said no. Several days later, a guard escorted me to the Office of Internal Affairs. A captain, investigator, and several counselors were waiting for my arrival. The investigator asked, "Why didn't you inform us of all your relatives who are employed here." I told them that information was provided during my pre-sentencing report. The investigator countered, "Your cousin notified us." I did not believe him and thought the comment was a smoke screen to cover the snitch. They told me that I would be transferred to another prison soon.

Within a week, I was loaded on a bus to the Wabash valley prison in Sullivan County. For some reason, when the bus entered that facility, I had an overwhelming feeling of impending doom. I had presumed that they were going to send me back to the Indiana state prison. A counselor escorted me into an office within the core, an area in their cellhouses where all weapons are stored, where all movement is electronically controlled. The counselor explained the rules and procedures, and then assigned me to a cell block. When I asked for my allotment of state envelopes, he went into another office and returned with a stack of ten envelopes. He handed them to me and said I owed them on next month's allotment. I told him the transfer prevented me from receiving my allotment at Pendleton. The counselor abruptly snatched the envelopes from my hand, lacerating a finger in the process. "Look coon, I'm doing you a favor," he said. When I looked up, I saw a guard standing on a glass ceiling above me. His pistol pointed at my head. The counselor said convicts sent to that prison are classified as recalcitrant and unwanted at other prisons.

They assigned me to a cell with a middle-aged black sociopath, the first person sentenced under Indiana's "three-strikes-you're-out" law. His third felony came from stealing a package of lunch meat. After I moved my property into the cell, the sociopath was called to the counselor's office for over an hour. That told me enough about him.

The cellhouses at the Indiana state prison and Pendleton reformatory had one-man cells. This place forced you to share that small space with another convict. It was my first time in this situation. This type of arrangement leads to interpersonal contempt and violence. When my cellmate returned from his meeting with prison officials, his demeanor toward me turned to cold indifference. I knew that white society had mastered manipulating Black people to conflict with each other.

A month later, they transferred me to another cell block where I bunked with a severely disturbed juvenile thug. He was in his early twenties and appeared to have extremely low self-esteem and depression. There were days he went without taking a shower or brushing his teeth. He just laid there staring at the ceiling all day. His gym shoes smelled of ammonia from the fungal rot. He displayed contempt because they assigned me to the lower bunk. He delighted in placing those funky-ass gym shoes under the bed right under where I lay. He was in a gang. When his boys were present, he acted like a completely different person. He said most of his life was spent in various homes and juvenile prisons. One day, he pulled out a white photo album to show me pictures of his family. However, there were only photographs of white males. It raised a red flag to me: why didn't this black male have photos of black people in his album? Why did he join a black street gang? I had a hunch that he was an informant and that one-day, white folks would throw him to the dogs.

During recreation, his gang crew held meetings in the cell. I usually took reading material and left the area. The prison had a rule that if contraband was found in a cell, both occupants would face the same consequence. His antisocial personality traits came out in the presence of his friends. I paid special attention to one of his activities: after each meal, the cellblock was locked down. However, they would open our cell door electronically to let him leave the cell block to meet with police for at least thirty minutes every day. No other convict had this type of routine. I noticed him always having a private conversation with the Sergeant-in-charge. After one secret meeting with the police, he came back to the cell and showed me a sandwich bag full of light-pink chips. "This is crack cocaine. I am selling it for the police," he said.

I was reading the New Yorker magazine when this young thug entered the cell with six gang members and told me to get another cellmate. He said that one of his crew wanted to share the cell with him. I had no problem and waited until recreation was over and remained seated in the dining area. The officer-in-charge entered the unit with several guards and asked if I had a problem. I asked for a different cell assignment, but they told me to find someone that would switch cells with me. Everyone that I asked refused. This placed me in a conflictual circumstance with that sociopath.

There was a white, ex-cop in the cell block. He was serving an eighty-year prison sentence for murder. He killed a man during a drug transaction. His job assignment was cleaning cell block showers after each recreation period. I noticed the cop and my cellmate started having daily meetings. One day, I was the last person in line waiting to take a shower. Once I entered the shower, the ex-cop stood in front of the bars and told me not to splash soap on the walls. I said, "Motherfucker, are you a punk?" We exchanged insults and other diatribes. I knew we were going to be trading blows after that verbal encounter.

After my shower, I returned to the cell, but my cellmate had locked down with someone else. I looked in the dining area and saw black gang members whispering to the ex-cop. My intuition told me to go put on my gym shoes and prepare for battle. The ex-cop walked up to my cell and waved his arm at the guard tower. A white female guard in the control tower electronically opened my cell door and then suddenly disappeared. The ex-cop entered my cell and closed the door; I immediately ran off a combination of three punches to his face – called a "three-piece." We traded punches, but my arm length was much longer and that kept him at bay. He tried a police tactic of going low to grab my legs and throw me backward. It didn't work. He busted his forehead after a failed attempt trying to head-butt me. He got up holding his head, then pulled out a fourteen-inch butcher knife from the kitchen, "The guards gave me this to kill you," he said.

They transferred me to another cell block where I was given a job cleaning the dining room seats. Ms. Minor was the only Black woman guard employed at the prison. She was the officer-in-charge (OIC) of the unit. It was rumored that she was in the middle of a nasty divorce. I asked her why there was so much hostility directed at me in that prison. Her reply shocked me. "You are Dr. Van Johnson, a psychiatrist who killed a white man in Anderson. That white man belonged to a secret society that many white officers and staff at this prison are also members of. The white folks knew you were going to be transferred to this prison and held a meeting to plan your demise. They created all sorts of lies and false information about you. You will be alienated from the population and then murdered. It is about revenge."

I had to quickly produce a strategy or otherwise be killed in that prison. I knew that all mail entering or leaving the prison was monitored, evaluated, and copied by staff. However, legal mail was the only exception. Since this plot involved prison authorities, I decided to send a letter labeled "Legal Mail" directly to the Governor of Indiana. The staff would be hesitant to open or destroy mail addressed to the governor. The letter detailed everything that Officer Minor had told me.

They transferred me to a cell with the most violent black psychopath in the prison. This beast had recently beat up his own cousin that shared the cell. Every day, he made veiled threats of violence, however, I knew that any response would make things worse. I thought, "This is the nigger who is going to kill me."

According to the DSM manual of psychiatry, this Bat-Turd that I was now housed with had a classic case of "Intermittent Explosive Disorder." Simply put, he is the kind of person offended by the smallest slights, or perceived transgressions. He may or may not say anything at that time of a perceived insult. But he would still hold those hostile thoughts and emotions toward the person. Then unexpectedly, he explodes into violence against the perceived person that offended him.

Every night, I slept with one eye open. I had no idea when this nightmare would end. One afternoon before lunch, two white men in black suits appeared in front of the cell door hatch. One of them kneeled in front of the hatch and asked for Mr. Johnson. When I came to the door, they flashed gold badges and said they were special investigators from the governor's office. They asked if I knew the whereabouts of officer Minor. I pointed to the adjacent cell block where I saw her working earlier that day. The investigators rushed to the cellblock. Several days later, two men, one black and one white entered the cell house through a back door at approximately 2:39 a.m. They were wearing some type of jumpsuits I never saw before. They came directly to my cell and told me to pack up my property because I was being transferred to another prison. Once I dragged my four boxes of property out of the cell, the officers carried them through the back door, and placed them in a white DOC station wagon parked outside. The operation was conducted quickly while most of the convicts were asleep. They escorted me out of the building without handcuffs or leg shackles. Once we were outside of the building, the black officer smoked a cigarette before we got into the vehicle. Once we cleared the check points in the prison complex and was on the outside, the black officer told me, "The order to immediately transfer you came directly from the governor's office. We had to get you out of there with the quickness." I arrived back at the Indiana state prison three hours later at sunrise.

Chapter Ten

THIS TIME, JUDGE SPENCER APPOINTED ATTY. ROBERT Rock, Jr. as my pauper appellate counsel on direct appeal. Outside of owning several Wendy's franchises in Anderson, he unsuccessfully ran for Mayor of Anderson and state representative. It was alleged that he inherited the businesses from his late father, Robert Rock, Sr. The latter was a wealthy owner of a car dealership in Anderson; a state representative; Lt. governor of Indiana; and former mayor of Anderson.

Atty. Robert Rock, Jr. was not politically correct to prepare my direct appeal. What I heard about him from folks I cannot name scared the daylights out of me. His father was allegedly in the KKK. He did not need the little money the court paid for pauper appeals. So, why did Spencer appoint him?

Atty. Rock sent me a standard letter indicating his appointment as my counsel on direct appeal. He invited me to contact his office if I had any questions. His phone number and address were listed. I wrote his office and tried to call several times. However, his office never responded to any of my written inquiries, or ever accepted a collect from me!

I had my suspicions and decided to call attorney David Stone, IV. I figured that since both were in the appellate business in the same community, they knew each other. My hunch was correct. Atty. Stone gave me some valuable information about him. "I contacted Atty. Robert Rock and informed him that I had prepared the first direct appeal, knew the case thoroughly, and would do the direct appeal free of charge. Atty. Rock refused my request to do the appeal, and said that he had to bury the case, for the last time." Now, that is an ear full! I was told that Spencer was a Klansman, and wondered if Rock was also one—his father was allegedly one.

The appellate court only reviews what is on the face of the trial record on direct appeal. A conviction will be upheld on direct appeal if an issue is incorrectly, or falsely presented, if new evidence was not presented at trial. Constitutional issues are deemed waived if not raised on direct appeal!

In the fall of 1997, I received a copy of Atty. Robert Rock's blue book, his appellate brief filed with the Indiana court of appeals. The issues he raised were unbelievable.

Issue 1.) <u>Did the defendant's trial counsel render ineffective assistance of counsel?</u>

Issue 2.) <u>Did the trial court abuse its discretion when it denied the requests of the defendant for a new attorney?</u>

Issue 3.) <u>Did the prosecutor engage in prosecutorial misconduct so as to place the defendant in grave peril and improperly prejudice the defendant's right to a fair trial?</u>

The Indiana appellate court upheld the conviction. All three issues raised by Atty. Rock were designed to fail! I will discuss the three issues:

Issue 1.) Atty. Rock noted that Oliver, the defense counsel, was responsible for my appearance in jail clothes at trial: Atty. Oliver didn't take advantage of the court's offer for a recess to purchase his client's clothing. Ironically, Rock failed to mention Oliver's written "Objection" to my appearance at trial in jail clothes. He failed to note the court refused to release any money for clothing, despite the fact Oliver said he would accept a much lesser amount than requested.

In all fairness, Rock was not aware that my motion for mistrial at Voir dire was somehow deleted from the court record. In doing that, it gave a false depiction that the jury was not present when the police brought me into the courtroom.

Atty. Rock failed to note that Oliver did not notify the court I had no clothing for trial, prior to the 5/26/1996 deadline. Atty. Oliver failed to move for a mistrial on the issue. Once the jury saw me in jail clothes, a recess would not have restored my presumption of innocence. You cannot "unwring" a bell, so to speak. The court should have sustained my motion for a mistrial, dismissed and replaced the entire jury pool, provided me with money for civilian clothes, and started a new trial.

Atty. Rock failed to raise the issue that Atty. Oliver withheld new evidence at trial by not subpoenaing Mr. James Ericksen's to testify at trial. His sworn statement was entered into the court record at arraignment. It is the jury's responsibility to weigh all evidence in a case. Atty. Oliver foreclosed the jury from fulfilling its responsibility.

Issue 2.) Atty. Rock raised this inappropriate issue on direct appeal. Yes, I did file a complaint against Atty. Montague Oliver Jr. with the Indiana supreme court disciplinary commission. The commission opened an investigation but took no adverse action against his license to practice law. This issue had absolutely nothing to do with the trial process. There was absolutely no reason for making this an issue on direct appeal, or any stage of the appellate process!

Issue 3.) Atty. Rock noted that the prosecutor made comments in the final argument that rose to the level of official misconduct. But he failed to illustrate the specific statement(s), or their location in the record of proceedings (transcripts). Every defendant at trial is placed in jeopardy of grave peril by the nature of being charged with a criminal offense. If the state erred by presenting false statements during a final argument, the normal course of action is a motion for mistrial by the defense. Even if the motion is denied, the issue is preserved for appellate review. Final arguments are a summary of the state's theory of the case, supported by facts already presented. But the arguments are not considered evidence in themselves. Prosecutorial Misconduct is rarely presented on direct appeal. It was inappropriate and unsupported by any facts in the trial record in this case. A defendant cannot receive relief if a claim is unsupported by fact.

Prosecutorial misconduct is when the prosecution has used altered or fabricated evidence to obtain a criminal conviction. That is exactly what happened in this case. Rock received information that the state used altered evidence to obtain the conviction. His job was to inappropriately present this issue on direct appeal. Why? The powers-to-be in Anderson knew that one day I would get a copy of the court transcripts of my trial. I would discover that the police had altered the decedent's attire; re-arranged furniture and other items in my home and planted a newspaper next to the dead body. Rock knew that if he inappropriately presented the issue on direct appeal, the doctrine of Res Judicata prevented me from correctly raising the issue in a petition for post-conviction relief. This is big time corruption!

Atty. Rock failed to raise the issue that the court abused its discretion by Sua sponte instructing the jury on self-defense over the objection of defense counsel.

Atty. Rock failed to raise the issue that the court failed to protect my fifth amendment right against Double Jeopardy.

Atty. Rock successfully carried out his duty to squash my direct appeal, and let the system bury me in prison.

Chapter Eleven

THANKS TO ROCK, MY CONVICTION WAS AFFIRMED AT EVERY level of the appellate process. After a direct appeal is denied review in the U.S. Supreme court, the appellate attorney is required to notify the defendant about the deadline to file a petition for post-conviction relief. However, Rock never notified me about anything. As a result, I filed the petition past the deadline, which barred it from being litigated in federal court where res judicata is not an automatic bar to review a case.

At the time, I was unaware of any other way to challenge that wrongful conviction. I went into a deep depression. Those Hoosiers of Anderson gave me a lesson in White Power! A prison law clerk asked if I had ever read the transcripts from my trial. "You don't really know what happened in your case until those transcripts are studied," he said. The clerk helped me prepare a motion to receive a copy of my transcripts from the Indiana supreme court. After submitting that motion, the Indiana supreme court ordered the court clerk to send me a copy of the record of proceedings in my trial.

The court sent ten boxes of transcripts to the Indiana state prison. Several law clerks had to help me transport the twenty-four volumes of records to my cell. A law clerk said that my second conviction could be challenged with a petition for post-conviction relief. I filed a petition and checked the box requesting legal counsel from the Indiana public defender's office. They assigned one of their top attorneys to my case. She wrote that it would be at least two years before she could review my case.

A year later, the state public defender came to see me at the Indiana state prison. She got right to the point. "Mr. Johnson, the lawyer who did your direct appeal destroyed the case! He inappropriately raised issues on direct appeal normally raised on post-conviction relief like, 'the ineffective assistance of trial counsel.' He waived issues by incorrectly presenting them with arguments backed by no evidence in the trial record, and without controlling case law. There were many issues with constitutional merit, but he destroyed them all on direct appeal." She said there were no issues of fundamental error that could be raised in the petition for post-conviction relief. "I'm barred from re-litigating waived issues, those incorrectly presented, or lacking evidence under the doctrine of collateral Estoppel or *Res Judicata*," she said. I asked if those issues and deficiencies could be raised under "Ineffective assistance of appellate counsel?'" She replied, "Issues of fundamental error cannot be raised in a post-conviction petition. There is nothing that can be done now. I know the appellate lawyer did not inform you that a post-conviction petition had to be filed within a year after the U.S. supreme court denied his writ of certiorari. If you had filed the petition within that period, I could've appealed this case in the federal court where Res Judicata is not an absolute bar to correction."

I took the time to carefully review the transcripts of my trial. The law clerk was correct about not knowing what happened until the transcripts are reviewed. I discovered that Oliver had filed a 'Notice of Appearance' as my attorney on June 1, 1990. The first time I met Atty. Oliver was on Monday, June 11, 1990, while in the county jail, a day after my arrest. We were total strangers when he filed that fraudulent document in the Madison circuit court. Someone had to secretly pay him, because that document was not filed as a 'Pro Bono' appearance. But Oliver claimed that the police allowed him into my home because he was volunteering legal services on my behalf. The big question is, "Did officials at St. John's hospital pay him through a proxy for the purpose of obtaining my banking and business transactions? After Wagner had killed me, was Oliver the designated media spokesperson? Since the contract Hit did not work out as planned, how much did Oliver assist the police in re-staging the setting of my home? Why didn't Chavis disclose how Oliver sabotaged my legal defense?

The transcripts revealed that Anderson police allowed Mrs. Jan Wagner, the decedent's wife, into my apartment on the night of the shooting. She contacted R. Knuckles, an off-duty Anderson police officer, who sent his wife and some lady to drive her home. Why did she need to call an off-duty Anderson police officer, while plenty of them were already in my home? Unbeknownst to me at the time, Atty. William Lawler, the Madison County prosecutor, lived in my housing complex. He was present with the other police in my home. What role did he play in the alteration of evidence in my home?

In the middle of the eighth volume of transcripts, there were black-and-white photocopies of the interior of my home. This is where I got the shock of my life. Mr. Wagner's body was staged with his head positioned near a marble end table in front of the couch. An Anderson Herald Bulletin newspaper was placed next to his head but would be upside down to anyone sitting on the couch. There was no newspaper in that home before the police took me to the station! My housekeepers thoroughly cleaned the home within twenty-four hours of the shooting. I had an out-of-town guest arriving on Monday morning. The police planted that newspaper next to Wagner's head to visually reinforce their contrived alibi that he came there to collect a newspaper debt. Not one person at trial stated the amount I owed on a newspaper debt. There was no debt!

Photos showed Wagner dressed in a light-colored shirt with no black powder residue, blue jeans, and unlaced white gym shoes. When Wagner attacked me, he was wearing a blue fur-lined winter overcoat, yellow polo shirt, blue jeans, and brown lizard-skin cowboy boots. However, after the shooting, a black powder residue covered an area over the chest region on the overcoat. If Wagner did not have on that overcoat, his shirt would've been covered with that black powder residue. During an interview with a news reporter, Lt. Richwine said that Wagner was shot at near point-blank range. It was proof that the police removed his overcoat. Who would wear a fur-lined winter overcoat on a warm summer night?

I usually kept my personal records in a suitcase in the main closet. Police scattered those records around the decedent's legs and feet, which were staged in the foreground of the photo, near my fireplace. The police did that to make the planted newspaper near his head appear normal among a field of scattered debris. One photo showed where police placed an open psychiatry textbook on a stool next to my bookshelves. They placed it there to raise doubts about my story of listening to music when I noticed Wagner standing in front of my bedroom window. Reading a textbook requires lighting, which would contradict my claim of listening to music with the lights off in my home.

The bar in my den had four bar stools. The transcript photograph showed only one stool sitting in front of it. The Sony stereo system was shown sitting in the entrance of the guest restroom. My extensive album collection was kept in a series of milk crates on the floor of the closet. In the photo, the milk crates were now lined up in two rows in front of the bookshelves and extended to the den's window. Police did this to fictionalize my story that, "I was sitting in front of the stereo, which was in front of the window, listening to music with headphones when Wagner suddenly appeared standing in front of the window." Of course, that could not be true if the stereo is sitting at the entrance of the restroom; with the crates of albums sitting in front of the window. Their intent was to create the perception that it was impossible for me to be listening to music and simultaneously facing the window.

One photo showed a police officer holding open a large trash bag. I bet that is where they placed the decedent's overcoat and cowboy boots for disposal.

Why had Anderson police altered and planted evidence in my home? Police canvassed the housing complex after the shooting. One neighbor claimed that James Wagner came to her residence about an hour before the shooting. She said he had on a light-colored shirt, blue jeans, and white gym shoes. However, Wagner's attire was quite different when the police arrived at my home. This discrepancy in his appearance at two separate locations just yards apart, would've contradicted the contrived alibi they made up to account for his presence at my home. So,

THE LEGAL LYNCHING OF A BLACK PSYCHIATRIST

the police had to resolve that dilemma by removing Wagner's overcoat and replacing his cowboy boots with the white gym shoes, which they forgot to lace up one of the shoestrings.

The motive for altering the evidence in my home? The goal was to make my account of what led up to the shooting appear fictional.

The outcome would have been different had I been shown this evidence prior to trial. My defense team did not even subpoena my two housekeepers to testify at trial.

The Indiana state medical examiner performed a forensic autopsy on James Wagner. His testimony and the official autopsy report were not part of the trial Transcripts. But why? This was done to avoid disclosing Wagner's toxicology profile! The transcripts revealed that a statement by Atty. Oliver at Voir Dire of the second trial was deleted from the record by Spencer to protect Oliver from disbarment: Oliver falsely claimed that my family had taken responsibility for providing my clothing at the second trial. I rebutted that claim at trial. If not, it would have remained in the record and absolved the court of all responsibility in that issue. Yet, in his motion for expenses prior to trial, Oliver said, "Mr. Johnson is estranged and lacked support from his family."

Reading those transcripts took me to another dimension. To add insult to injury, one day I was having lunch in the chow hall when a guy named Don Mitchell walked through the chow line. I knew he was from Anderson because I always saw him at the black nightclubs. He told me that the Madison County prosecutor convicted him of sales and distribution of narcotics; and sentenced him to thirty years in prison. He immediately recognized me and came over to the table and sat down. He said that Atty. Oliver was a crackhead and responsible for me being in prison. Then told me an unforgettable story about Atty. Oliver. "I was bagging up some heroin when Oliver and his white secretary came to my home. He purchased an eight-ball of crack cocaine, which cost $500 dollars. They borrowed a crack pipe and smoked the entire quantity on my couch. When they finished, Oliver asked for another eight-ball. I asked for the money. He said I would get paid when he got his public defender check. I reminded him that my business was cash on demand.

The white girl abruptly took off all her clothes and stood by the front door naked, so that all my customers would see that she was for sale; selling that ass to get some crack."

In December 2006, I filed a petition for post-conviction relief, despite knowing that Atty. Rock had waived all the constitutional issues in the case. My goal was to make a permanent record of how the police and prosecutor used altered and planted evidence to convict me. It would also disclose how the court and defense team colluded with the police and state to railroad me into prison. I raised four issues: 1) The court violated my right to due process by compelling me to stand trial in jail clothes. 2) The state used altered and planted evidence in my home at trial to obtain a conviction. It violated my right to due process and a fair trial. 3) ineffective assistance of appellate counsel: Atty. Rock failed to raise the issue that trial counsel withheld newly discovered evidence at trial. 4) ineffective assistance of appellate counsel: Rock failed to raise the issue that Oliver failed to challenge the presence of an all-white male jury at trial.

April 2007, I filed a motion to produce all photographic evidence, which included the crime scene videotape. Judge Spencer denied that motion without cause. A hearing was scheduled in August 2008. Atty. Cummins of Delaware county was appointed the special prosecutor. This was done because Atty. Thomas Broderick, Jr., my former defense attorney, was now the Madison County prosecutor. It would have been perceived as a conflict of interest if Broderick represented the state against his former client. The court did not note the nature of the hearing. I presumed that it was an evidentiary hearing. It was something else.

I subpoenaed former defense Atty. Chavis, appellate counsel Atty. Rock, Mrs. Jan Wagner, James Nave, the chief deputy prosecutor, and some of the police investigators on my face sheet.

I was transferred to the Madison County detention center several days before the hearing. On the day of the hearing, I was escorted into the courtroom at 8:50 am, an hour earlier than scheduled. A deputy removed my handcuffs and leg shackles for the small crowd of black spectators in the auditorium. I sat at a table next to the special prosecutor. A copy of James Ericksen's sworn statement was on the table in front of us.

Chavis was the only person who appeared at the hearing. We had a professional relationship and personal friendship. Because Chavis did not represent me at the second trial, he could now testify as a witness at the hearing. He could discuss the various excuses Nave gave him for failing to provide the crime scene photographs and crime scene videotape under his motion for discovery—a serious Brady Violation. This was an opportunity to expose how Atty. Oliver destroyed and sabotaged my case.

Chavis entered the courtroom and sat next to me at the table with Atty. Cummins. Minutes later, Spencer entered the courtroom and noticed Chavis seated next to me, and asked, "Why did you summon Atty. Chavis to appear at this hearing?"

I responded, "Chavis had been to my home on numerous occasions and knew the layout. Atty. Nave, the deputy chief prosecutor, repeatedly gave him excuses for not turning over the pictorial and crime scene videotape evidence. I never saw the state's evidence prior to the trial. The defense team never reviewed or vetted the evidence with me. He can also describe how Atty. Oliver sabotaged my defense."

Judge Spencer appeared angry. Then he told Chavis, "We do not need you at this hearing. You can go back to Indianapolis." Chavis slowly rose from his chair and walked towards the back exit, but before exiting he stood near the door and stared at Spencer with disgust. I already knew that the post-conviction court could not grant relief on issues waived on direct appeal. Spencer could have just null-and-voided my petition on a lack of merit and avoided a hearing altogether. Why did he schedule that hearing? At some level, did Spencer understand my reasoning for filing that petition? Granting a hearing gave the petition a degree of legitimacy and it became a permanent record – my strategy. Over 96% of post-conviction petitions are dismissed outright. Rarely does a court grant a hearing.

When Spencer brought the court to the session, the special prosecutor addressed the court. "Your honor, I move for a dismissal of this petition because it contains issues already litigated under similar themes, which is a violation of the doctrine of Res Judicata." The court made no ruling at that time. I then moved the court for a production of the crime scene photographs and videotape. Then came a shocking revelation from Spencer that shook up everyone in the courtroom. "Mr. Johnson, all that evidence in your case has disappeared. We looked everywhere and could not find it. Look, you beat a murder rap and your conviction was overturned. 'In the first place, why didn't you just leave Anderson?"

I responded, "Your honor, I had recently opened a new office in Indy and did not know I had a time limit on moving out of Anderson. Everything you mentioned involved the first trial and appeal. I thought this hearing was about the events that took place during the second trial. I do not want to be branded a felon for the rest of my life to satisfy this town's thirst for revenge."

Oliver sauntered into the courtroom. After identifying himself, he said, "I'm no longer practicing law." When I pressed for more information, Oliver refused to divulge the reason for not practicing law.

Spencer spoke on his behalf. "Mr. Oliver's situation has nothing to do with this matter. He doesn't have to answer that question." A prison law clerk gave me a copy of the Indiana supreme court's disciplinary action against Oliver. They suspended his license for cheating a client out of money.

Ericksen's affidavit was on the table in front of me and the special prosecutor. I asked Oliver why he did not subpoena Mr. Ericksen to testify at trial. He said, "I was unaware of that affidavit."

I asked, "How could you have been unaware when the judge read excerpts from that document at the arraignment?" Atty. Oliver sat there in silence. I asked Oliver, "Why didn't you let the court know I had no clothing for trial before the May 29, 1996, deadline?"

Atty. Oliver answered, "A sheriff deputy told me that you didn't mind going to trial in jail clothes." I asked, "What's the deputy's name? Did you get an affidavit from him?"

Atty. Oliver answered, "I don't remember his name and didn't get an affidavit."

I asked, "Is that why you didn't move the court for a mistrial at Voir dire?"

Oliver did not answer the question. Spencer asked Oliver, "Was the jury present during our discussion about Mr. Johnson's attire at trial?"

Atty. Oliver responded, "Yes, they were present." The special prosecutor shook his head as he looked at the floor. At that point, Atty. Cummins could have moved the court in the interest of justice to vacate my conviction, but he did not.

Spencer then tried to flip the script on me. "Mr. Johnson, why didn't you say something then? If you sit there and say nothing in court, you cannot come back with that issue."

I responded, "Your honor, do not forget you denied my motion for mistrial and told me to sit down and shut up. I filed an affidavit to that effect."

Spencer ignored my rebuttal and adjourned the court for lunch. As spectators were leaving Spencer glanced at the court reporter as she gathered her belongings. The female deputy guarding me also left the courtroom. That left Judge Spencer and me alone in the courtroom. He walked up to me and pointed at the court reporter and whispered, "She is the wife of Detective Ward, the Anderson detective you subpoenaed to testify at this hearing. Do not be surprised at the type of record you get from this proceeding." It was a conflict of interest for her to be in that courtroom during this hearing! Detective Ward was on the board of The Church of God, headquartered at Anderson college. In an odd way, Spencer was letting me know that he was aware that the police had framed me.

When the court was brought into session after lunch, Spencer revealed his attitude towards me. "Dr. Johnson, I always liked you. You have done a lot of good, and then this one situation. I believed what the state trooper told you. The only thing that angered me was your reference to Mr. Wagner as a motherfucker." I tried to explain to Spencer the nuances of that word in black culture. Spencer said I did not raise the right issue of fundamental error and that he could grant me leave to re-submit a petition with the correct issue. I declined because the state public defender told me that there was no relief for issues of fundamental error in the post-conviction court. White folks think Black people are dumb. He repeatedly asked if I wanted leave to submit another petition. The reason he wanted me to withdraw that petition. A new petition automatically discharges the previous petition from the record. None of the information contained in the old petition can reappear in a subsequent petition. In the addendum section of that petition, I detailed how St. John's hospital lured me to Anderson, forced me to sign insurance policies with them as beneficiary, requested me to commit insurance fraud, the state trooper's warning about the hit on my life, the illegal wiretaps on my office phone, and Ericksen's affidavit about James Wagner. In other words, the whole nine yards, so to speak.

At the time of the hearing, my earliest release date was in seven months. If I had filed a new petition, Spencer would have taken no action before my release. Once I had gained my freedom, the court would have said that I got relief by being set free. This disregards the lifelong stigma of "felon."

I raised several issues in the petition under ineffective assistance of appellate counsel. However, at the hearing, Spencer said Atty. Robert Rock, Jr. had relocated to Evansville, Indiana. "I didn't think his testimony warranted the time and travel to this hearing," he said. I was disappointed. "Your honor, I disagree with your disposition about him not being at this hearing. He was the court-appointed pauper appellate counsel for my direct appeal and waived every issue of merit. He purposely destroyed my case. Is that why you appointed him?" I would have loved to stare Rock in the eyes and ask him who gave the orders to destroy my appeal.

Judge Spencer said that he did not subpoena Mrs. Jan Wagner, the decedent's wife, because she moved to Florida. I told the court that she helped the police frame me. "On the night of the shooting, she came into my home and claimed that her husband's wedding band was missing. Her allegation resulted in a search warrant for my home. No wedding band was found, "I said.

Judge Spencer subpoenaed Anderson's police officers to testify at the hearing. But most of them were not on the force when the shooting occurred in 1990. Detectives Rodney Cummings, John Ward, and Lt. Richwine were not subpoenaed to testify. They supervised the processing of my home on the night of the shooting. The police were well rehearsed on what to say and followed the script well. I made an unknowing tactical mistake by not motioning the court for the separation of witnesses prior to the start of the hearing. They sat together in a section of the courtroom. One-by-one, they took the witness stand and repeated in rote fashion, the identical answers to every question. When I showed them photocopies of my apartment, all of them claimed that the pictures were "blurry and unclear." They denied any recollection of seeing an overcoat or cowboy boots. I knew they would lie. However, if they were not questioned about that issue, the court would have ruled it moot—the lies gave permanence to the issue. The fact that Spencer compelled them to take time out of their busy schedules meant something. They were aware that I knew they had framed me, and so did Spencer.

Detective Kevin Smith supervised the processing of evidence in my home on the night of the shooting. When he entered the courtroom, Spencer greeted him like an old friend. "Officer Smith was mayor of Anderson from 2000-2004." He then pointed to a large portrait on the wall, "That is the judge who passed this gavel to me. He presided in this courtroom for many years before retiring. That is officer Smith's father."

Spencer addressed Officer Smith, "I want to congratulate you on the promotion of your brother, Atty. Steven Smith, to the position of clerk of the Indiana Court of Appeals and Supreme court." Prior to taking the witness stand, the special prosecutor coached Detective Smith on what words to use, and not use when answering my questions. What was the purpose of Spencer revealing that much information about officer Smith's background? He was showing me the extensive network of some powerful white people responsible for me being in prison.

Officer Smith was polite and answered with basic identifying information. But, when questioned about his role in the handling of the evidence, he repeatedly answered, "I have no recollection whatsoever of that case." He repeated that phrase to every question. I ended the interrogation.

The trial transcripts revealed that James Wagner's body was taken to the Madison County coroner prior to being transferred to the state medical examiner at Indiana university. What procedure(s) was conducted on the body prior to transfer to Indiana university? Spencer knew the issue had to be addressed. He pulled out a small flip phone in the courtroom and claimed to be calling the deputy coroner of Madison County. But was he in that position when my incident occurred? Spencer spoke into the phone without the speaker on, as if he were conversing with someone. The fact that he did not turn on the phone's speaker to verify the call was real and cast doubt about his claim of being on the phone talking to someone. Suddenly, he shouted, "the coroner said he has no knowledge of this case." Of course he did not. Because someone else held that position in 1990. There was loud whispering coming from the audience. Everyone knew it was a fraud.

Atty. Cummins asserted that there was drug involvement in the case. He started reading aloud Mr. Ericksen's affidavit about James Wagner's criminal history and substance abuse. The Judge countered. "There were no drugs involved in this case!" Only the state medical examiner knew what was in Wagner's blood, but he did not disclose it. The Anderson police did not collect a sample; defense Atty. Broderick did not question the medical examiner about Wagner's toxicology profile at trial. Even though the medical examiner's official report was not in the transcripts, I had a hunch that the special prosecutor knew where the skeletons were hidden.

At the conclusion of the hearing, Spencer said that I posed no threat to society, and he had no reason to block my release from prison in a few months. He made no ruling on the petition at that time but granted my motion to preserve all the trial and hearing records.

In April 2009, I received a memorandum from the Madison circuit court. Your petition for post-conviction relief was denied on the grounds of res judicata. I expected that type of decision. The hearing served several purposes: It exposed Atty. Oliver as being a sellout. I found out that the photographic and crime scene videotape evidence in my case was destroyed by someone. If they had a valid case, that evidence would not have disappeared. The court wanted me to file another petition so that key facts in that document would have been removed from the record and barred from being raised again in a subsequent petition.

Several weeks after I received the court memorandum, I received a copy of the transcripts from the post-conviction hearing. Judge Spencer warned me not to be surprised. I found numerous witness statements had been changed or deleted. There were large empty spaces where paragraphs were deleted and replaced with the caption, "inaudible, or couldn't understand." Key qualifying words in some sentences were changed and altered in the context of certain questions and responses, e.g., the word "was" had been changed to was not in a few sentences. Commas, colons, semicolons, and hyphens were improperly placed in some sentences and paragraphs. There were paragraphs structured like "word salads." The motive? Those distorted narratives of the events at the proceeding made me appear illiterate, at least. It was a sophisticated form of jurist subterfuge designed to conceal and distort evidence. What could one expect from a white court reporter married to a detective that helped frame a black doctor? It was a show of power. It proved that white supremacy could destroy any Black person, anywhere, anytime.

I prepared a motion titled, "Correct or Modify the Post-Conviction Evidentiary Hearing Transcript." The document was lengthy with a line-by-line comparative assessment and correction of the transcript from my meticulous notes at the evidentiary hearing. Judge Spencer denied my motion, which means he endorsed the fraud.

Prison officials requested the name and address of where I would be living when released from prison on parole. It was a one-year obligation in my case. My wealthy siblings and other relatives refused my request for temporary shelter. When I could not provide an address of domicile, prison officials informed me that I couldn't be released to the streets without somewhere to live. As a result, prison officials were mandated to transport me back to Anderson, the seat of Madison County. My criminal conviction originated in that town.

Mr. Thompson was the superintendent of Zone 3 at the Westville prison. I had never met him, but a guard told me that he wrote a pass for me to come to his office. When I arrived, he was very cordial and asked me to take a seat. Then he said, "Hey Doc, I thoroughly went through your case. Don't let those people get away with what they did to you in that small town." I asked him what I could do. He replied, "You expose them! Author a book that puts them on front street. That is what the media did to you." This came from a tall, clean shaven white man.

The staff said I had to take an updated photo of myself several weeks before being released. Copies of that photo would be sent to the various police agencies, the courts, and Indiana Department of Corrections. I signed a release form to receive a social security card and a copy of my medical records upon release. However, prison officials failed to provide me with either my medical records, or the social security card when released. Their motive? They Knew I had a medical degree and feared that I would file a medical malpractice lawsuit against them. They mis-diagnosed me with Gout and treated me with the drug allopurinol over several years. I later found out from a doctor that I never had the disease.

On May 18, 2009. They released me from the Westville minimum security correctional center. Curiously, I never appeared before a parole board. The DOC transport officer drove me to a halfway house in Anderson. But on this final long ride in a police vehicle, they did not put me in leg shackles and handcuffs. There were four of us black men in that transport van, on our way to freedom. The officer even stopped at a White Castle for us to get some food. When we reached Anderson, I was dropped off in front of a halfway house. In touring the facility, I noticed a lot of empty beds. However, the facility manager told me there was no available bed space. He made a call, and then handed me the phone. A lady identified herself as my parole officer and would be there to pick me up soon. A few minutes later, a casually dressed middle-aged white woman entered the lobby and told me to get my property. We hopped in her red jeep Cherokee and took off. She claimed to be the wife of the

Pendleton Reformatory superintendent, but never disclosed where I was being taken. All I know is that we were on a state road.

We were on that road for about twenty-five minutes before I noticed a "Welcome to Muncie" sign. The parole officer made a right turn, and we ended up in front of the Muncie Mission on Liberty Street. I never imagined living in a mission, but this place had to be the Ritz Carlton of missions. The campus was a block-long and contained a thrift store, warehouse, the main residential building (built like a German Castle), and an ornate administrative building. The dormitories, lecture rooms, classrooms, cafeteria, several libraries, and a recreation facility were in the main building.

The parole officer took me to meet Phil, the director of the men's program. She left after introducing us. Phil was a soft-spoken, clean-shaven white man in his late thirties. He was a former small-town cop that rose through the ranks to become a director at the mission. He discussed the rules at the facility and gave me a tour. He assigned me to the phase-one dorm.

At the time, I was the only Black resident living in the facility. The staff went out of their way to make me feel comfortable. Initially, the other white residents avoided me. I'm sure they were informed about my status as an ex-convict just released from prison. On the weekend Saturday that I arrived, there was nothing for me to do, so I spent time in the lobby and read the town's newspaper. As I started reading the obituary, there was a picture of a forty-year-old man who recently died of cancer. His name was James Scaife. When his next of kin was listed, I knew they were my cousins. I caught up with Phil before he left, and asked if he knew any members of the Scaife family. He said Rev. Leo Scaife Jr. sometimes held Thursday evening services for the residents. Phil gave me his phone number.

When I called and introduced myself, Leo picked me up and took me on a tour of Muncie. Then we went to his mother Mattie's home. When we arrived, his brothers Wayne, Robert and Louis were standing in the backyard talking to each other. After we all met, Mattie came out and introduced herself. Their father had passed away several years ago.

Reverend Leo Scaife Sr. and Mattie had seventeen children; two sets of twins; five boys and twelve females. They were all grown now. One of the daughters is the mother of NBA and Ball State University Hall of Famer Bonzi Wells. All the brothers worked at some capacity in law enforcement: Robert, the lead detective for the Muncie police Department; Wayne, a parole officer in Terra Haute; Louis, a juvenile unit chief at the Pendleton Reformatory.

Leo Jr. took me to his brother's funeral at the Union Baptist Church of Muncie. An ornate 6.5-million-dollar building with an attached dining hall. The Scaife family was instrumental in its construction. Reverend Leo Scaife Sr. had been the senior pastor for many years.

As I viewed James body, he could not have weighted more than seventy pounds. Leo Jr. said he died of throat cancer. They did not understand because he never smoked or drank. I felt their warmth despite the loss. After the services, the family went next door to the dining hall and had a nice sit-down repast. I did not know it at the time, but the funeral director buries the body without the family present.

I settled down into the routine of the mission. It was not bad. Everything was clean and well maintained. There were three hot meals every day. One evening, I noticed that after every meal, a crowd of white men gathered behind the residential building to smoke. A middle-aged, rough looking white guy named Ray, appeared to have the most influence over the group. One day, I walked up to the group and asked for a cigarette. Ray handed me one. He said aloud, "Doctor Johnson, they railroaded you to prison for self-defense." The other residents stood there quietly. I asked how he came to that conclusion about me. Ray said that he had relatives and friends who lived in Anderson. It seemed like once he made that known about me, the other white residents began interacting with me. The mission received used bicycles from the Muncie police. Every resident had one except me. After Phil gave me one, the others invited me to their day-long bike rides around Ball State University and the city. It was a lot of fun and great exercise. Summer was approaching. I started riding my bike to Ball State University and hanging out in their library.

Mr. Sexton ran the busy thrift store. He reminded me of those nerdy type guys you see on college campuses. He took a fondness to me and gave me the job of pricing furniture before it was placed in the show room. The facility collected used furniture, cleaned it up, and resold it. Since I did not know anyone in that community, during weekdays, I spent my after-work time in the library, several blocks from the mission. The officials at the mission did not give me any problems. I played the game because that stability was needed then. However, all the other residents were finding jobs and moving on. I knew the universe had to open a portal for me to move on as well.

The female parole officer in Anderson called and said my parole would be switched to Muncie, which is Delaware County. My new parole officer was a white male about my height. He knew my cousins Wayne and Robert; and knew the politics behind my case. He said there were far more dangerous people that they had to monitor than me. He said they would periodically call the Muncie Mission to check on me. Phil was an ex-cop who knew how to monitor people. I went to the parole office two times in eight months.

I contacted Rosie. She was still unmarried with no children and had moved back to Indianola, Mississippi. It was where she was born and raised. Her parents had once owned the only Black newspaper and bus company in town. Now, they had deceased and left the home to Rosie, who was now working on her doctorate thesis. Every evening, I would go to the library at the mission and spend hours on the phone with her. She asked if it was possible with my parole status to come there over the Thanksgiving weekend. I contacted my parole officer who gave me permission for the out-of-state visit. Rosie sent me a two-way ticket to Jackson, Ms. The first time I traveled on a plane in many years. Rosie and I had a wonderful time over that weekend. That trip helped clear up a lot of my false stereotypes about Mississippi and its people.

As time went on in the mission, some of the white folks started acting differently towards me, i.e., they were giving me hints to move on with my life. I had a feeling that after my parole ended in May 2010, I would find myself out on the streets, homeless and destitute! Some of the other white residents started arguments with me over small stuff. Example, I wanted to see a downhill skiing match on television, but it led to an argument. The white guys reported the incident to the authorities, who called me on the carpet about the incident. I saw the resentment building towards me.

When I mentioned it to Rosie, she became worried about my safety in that all-white environment. "Van, you are still on parole. They could stage you in a situation that would violate that parole status and have you sent back to prison." She was correct. Any type of arrest by police could be considered a parole violation. Rosie called my parole officer, and they discussed the matter.

In January 2010, the parole board granted me permission to fulfill the remaining five months of parole at Rosie's home in Mississippi. Rosie's cousin, Betty King, sent me a one-way plane ticket to Jackson, Mississippi. When my flight arrived, Rosie picked me up for the two-hour drive to Indianola. Her parents left her a spacious three-bedroom ranch-style home with a den and library. A gardener tended to the half-acre grounds.

I had not spoken with my great aunt Lottie in a long time. She had retired and lived in Oak Park, Illinois. She was my mentor, family historian, and Flora's sister. I wondered if she had ever heard about this one-horse southern town. When I called her, I posed the question, "I bet you can't guest where I'm living?' She did not say anything. I said, "Indianola, Mississippi."

She replied, "What? You have relatives in that town. My parents lived in a town called Itta Bina, close to there." That floored me. She started giving me their names and phone numbers.

When I asked Rosie if she knew anyone on that list, she laughed and said, "I graduated from high school with two of your cousins. Lindell, my sister-in-law, is one of your cousin's aunts. Your cousin Emma taught elementary school and was my mother's seamstress. They all graduated from Mississippi Valley State University." Rosie looked at me said, "We need to stop asking questions before we find out that we're related." She took me to the homes of my distant relatives.

One day, Rosie took me to the home of Dr. and Mrs. Horn in Greenwood. Both were retired tenured professors at Mississippi Valley State University in Itta Bena, Ms. (He was a music professor and director of their march band. His wife was a Literature professor.) Dr. Horn was delighted to meet me. He talked about seeing my aunt Lottie at all the Church of God conventions and retreats. I wondered how he knew that Lottie was my aunt. This was my first time meeting him. Then he reminisced about the days in his youth, when he took my great-grandparents (Lottie's parents) to church every Sunday morning in the town of Itta Bena. He showed me a yearbook with Rosie's photo. She had completed three years at Mississippi Valley State University. It was an eventful evening.

Aunt Lottie mentioned that her aunt, Mary Lyle, had owned the only black floral shop in Indianola. When I told Rosie, she drove me to an intersection and pointed to the remnants of a building that once existed. She said, "People called her Mae Lyle. When I was a child, me and my siblings used to buy candy and ice cream from her store." I was amazed at the family history I missed, but yet, gained by tragedy that occurred in the white world.

I wondered how Rosie lived alone in that big home. She was now in her forties and living off an inheritance. Her only challenge was to present her thesis and receive the Doctor of Education degree. Rosie was the vice-president of the Sunflower County democratic party. As such, we were invited to a lot of soirees, cookouts, and receptions. Every day, she took me on a tour of a different city or town. I especially liked the Elks club in Greenville.

We had several months of tranquility. I did not mind keeping the place clean. One day, a dark-gray pickup truck with tinted windows started parking in her driveway at about 7 p.m. every night. The driver never got out of the vehicle, and she refused to disclose his identity. She would take a liter of Gray Goose vodka, two glass shooters, and spend several hours in the truck. Her demeanor towards me became increasingly hostile. Sometimes in her drunken state, after hours in the truck, she comes in the house tell me to get out of her home! I had an idea of what was taking place. You cannot serve two masters! I had to swallow my tongue because I had no place to go.

I was happy when the month of May arrived. The Indiana Department of Corrections sent me a Certificate of Discharge. I no longer had an obligation to the state.

On Sundays, we would go to the Harlot Casino for brunch in Greenville. But I especially loved going to the Elks club there. I met many masons there. They treated me well. It did not make a difference if you were "three or four lettered." Everyone knew Rosie. Her best friend was a lady named Dot. The wife of a state senator who was a grand lodge office. Dot was an administrator at the regional hospital in Greenville. She told me the hospital had received a two-million-dollar grant for mental health services. She wanted to help me get on my feet by presenting seminars on mental health conditions that plagued the Black community. I would receive a stipend for giving lectures on various mental health disorders. One of the masons had planned to get me a job working as a Mill Rite at Uncle Ben's Rice plant in Greenville. They had planned a coming-out ceremony for me at the Elks club. At this soiree, I would be introduced and meet all the black elected officials, doctors, lawyers, judges, and business owners that were masons. Dot gave Rosie the time and date to bring me. But when that day arrived, Rosie refused to take me to the event. She said that once I moved to Greenville and started making money, I would hook up with someone else and move on from her. Her guilty consciousness was working on her. She caused me to miss an opportunity to make some money, create another social network; and obtain transportation.

When I informed my cousin Emma about the situation at Rosie's home, she said the man making those visits was Acie. His twin sons were students in her sixth-grade class. He was a married deputy sheriff that had an on-and-off tryst with Rosie for over ten years.

Things got worse as her nightly rendezvous with the deputy continued. One night, she came in drunk and said that Acie was bringing a few police friends over to throw me out. I was not surprised. For years, he had a comfortable routine of coming over after work, having a few drinks, and then screwing her brains out in that king size bed. Now, my presence forced him to get that ass in the stunt-limiting cab of a pickup truck.

When they transferred my parole to that state, my rap sheet was sent to every law enforcement agency in Mississippi. Acie saw my profile on their daily bulletins. He did not want a one-to-one encounter with me. That is why he mentioned bringing his friends. I was angry at the circumstance but had to give her credit for getting me out of Indiana.

She paid the bills, took me many places where I met a lot of new people. I entered her circle from a position of weakness. I appreciated having a place to live, despite the third-party interference.

We continued the ritual of having breakfast at the Huddle House on Rt 82. The breakfast was a community ritual of "gossip with pancakes."

One day surfing the internet I saw a photo of Cynthia, my college sweetheart. I sent her a message. She asked if I was her teenage sweetheart. After I told her who we worked for in college, she sent her phone number. Every day, we were on the phone for hours. We had not communicated for over thirty-five years. She was now an R.N. at the Veteran's hospital in Pineville, Louisiana; lived in a gated community in Alexandria, Louisiana.

I explained my circumstance. Cynthia replied, "Years ago, I heard what happened to you in that small town. You were lucky to escape with your life. Ten years ago, they found Dr. Clarence Burton dead in a rental car at the JFK airport in New York. He had been shot in the back of the head."

Since Rosie paid my cell phone bill, she had access to the phone log. She noticed that I spent a lot of time talking to someone with a Louisiana phone number. Rosie called the number. Cynthia explained her former relationship with me. Rosie started trashing me in every conceivable way, but her strategy failed. Cynthia told her, "I know he went to prison, but we had a perfect courtship, and didn't separate because of interpersonal conflicts." She asked Rosie, "If he's so bad, why are you living with him?" Cynthia planned for me to live with her. Rosie became indignant. I reminded her of that nightly tryst with the deputy. I now had an option to escape her disrespect.

I packed my boxes the night before departure. Early the next morning, Rosie woke me up early and prepared an elaborate breakfast—a rarity. She asked me not to move away. I pointed out the danger her affair presented to my safety. "Our relationship is toxic and dysfunctional. You are not going to change. It is time for me to move on with my life."

Emma parked her pickup truck in Rosie's driveway and helped load my property. We arrived just minutes before the bus departed from the station. I loved living in Mississippi and did not really want to leave. If I had gotten that job at Uncle Ben's Rice, I would have lived in Mississippi for the rest of my life. I loved the brotherhood there, bonding with my distant relatives gave me a sense of belonging, and I enjoyed all the positive experiences and events I attended at the Elks club in Greenville, Ms. Most of All, I missed the Ebony Club and B.B. King Museum in Indianola, Ms.

I finally arrived in Louisiana. My Trailway bus arrived in Alexandria at 2:00 a.m. Cynthia met me at the bus station in a leopard outfit. It took her Jeep just twenty minutes to reach the gated community. She clicked on a hand-held device and the two large bronze gates opened to allow entry. The two-bedroom condominium had walk-in closets, all the latest appliances, fireplace, and sundeck. A six-foot picket fence surrounded the entire complex.

Cynthia had been through two divorces and had two grown daughters that became certified dental hygienists. In her early forties, she was diagnosed with Lupus, an autoimmune disorder, and was on a cocktail of different medications. She chose to work the second shift to avoid prolonged exposure to sunlight, which exacerbated the condition. She was still beautiful and never lost her integrity or class. I had a good rapport with both daughters. One confided with me that Cynthia had not dated anyone in over ten years.

She did not want me to get a menial job. I got bored sitting around the house all day with nothing to do. We rarely went on a date anywhere. She preferred to cook. At night, she often woke up crying from pain in her bones. I agonized over her suffering. She had no idea that I was suffering from a depersonalization disorder, which is common in people who were incarcerated. However, I realized there was no cure for Lupus. She often told me that she wanted to die. Some nights her suffering made me weep. The only thing that I could do was provide emotional support for her. I helped with the custodial requirements around the house.

I wanted to get something going in my life because if Cynthia passed away it meant being homeless again. I called Betty King in New York. She gave me the phone number of an instructor at Grambling University. He told me about a job opening at a rehabilitation facility in Monroe. I discussed the idea of getting a job with Cynthia. She did not like it but allowed me to pursue the lead. It turned out to be a disaster and left me homeless in that town.

I went to the town of Grambling and met that instructor. His father was the longtime director of Grambling's marching band, and they named a music building after him. We went on a tour of the university and its surrounding all-Black town. I spent the night in a building that could have been a prop for a horror movie: it had no water or electricity. Spider webs and bugs were everywhere. I sat awake all night in a folding chair.

The next morning, we drove to the town of Monroe. The instructor never gave me any information about the job. I did not know if they hired felons or not. If they did not, I would have lied to get a full-time job. They interviewed me for over two hours. I told my story to the facility director and their board of directors. The facility specialized in caring for patients with Alzheimer's disease and late-stage dementia. I had the job until they asked, "Have you ever been convicted of a criminal offense?" I told the truth like a damn fool and did not get hired. As the board members were leaving, they all shook my hand. The last one said, "One day, I'll see your story on television."

I was now stuck in the town of Monroe without no money or place to live. The instructor dropped me off at the downtown bus terminal. However, on Sundays, the buses do not run in that town. He promised to keep my property in his garage until I found a home. The sunset was approaching. There was a Salvation Army shelter down the street from the bus terminal. They did not allow me in because it was after the 4:00 p.m. deadline. Just blocks away, there was a park with a four-lane overpass. After it got dark, I laid back against a concrete support pillar and fell asleep. A police flashlight awakened me. Police had surrounded me with their guns drawn. They asked if I was a fugitive. Then they said that it was against the law to sleep in the parks at night. They took me in for a background check. But I was not handcuffed. After they found out there were no warrants for my arrest, they took me to the Salvation Army shelter. The transient population had to leave the shelter at 8:00 a.m. and could not return until 4:00 p.m. All entry into the facility was barred after 6:00 p.m. The main downtown bus terminal was only a half-block away from the shelter. I spent my days touring the city by riding every bus route. Then I would hang around the bus terminal until 4:00 p.m.

The bus tours became boring. Then I started hanging out in the cafeteria at a nearby hospital. One afternoon, I was sitting in the cafeteria when a tall Black man wearing a lab coat purchased a lunch tray and sat alone. I walked up to his table and asked if I could join him. He gave me a gesture of approval. The doctor introduced himself and said some things that only an Alpha or Mason would recognize. Like myself, he was both. After showing me his D-Card, identified himself as a board-certified internist. I disclosed my educational background and dire plight. Then he asked, "If you graduated from Rush Medical College, do you know Dr. Jim Nichols?" I said that Jim was in the class above me and had a PhD in biochemistry before he entered med school. The doctor said that Dr. Nichols had recently passed away. "We have to first get you some employment," he said. But I never saw him again.

The fall season with its colder temperatures and the holiday season was fast approaching. I had not spoken with Cynthia for months. Surprisingly, she called and asked if I was ready to come home. I admitted defeat. She sent me money for a bus ticket and was waiting at the bus terminal for me to arrive in Alexandria. We had a great Christmas celebration with her daughters and grandchildren. Her cooking was something to shout about. We had a feast and opened gifts in front of the fireplace. She purchased some expensive gifts but placed "From Van to Cynthia" on them. She did not want her daughters to know my true plight. But after the holiday celebrations, she asked me to find somewhere else to live. I asked, "Why did you ask me to come back for the holidays?

"I wanted you by my side one last time. I am going to die from this disease in a few years," she said.

In January 2011, another door was mysteriously opened for me after Thelma, my 92-year-old aunt, had passed away. Tony, her youngest son called and said that they were planning her funeral in Charleston, Missouri. He said that my name was at the start and end of Thelma's obituary. The family would send me a bus ticket to get to Charleston.

My aunt's funeral was well-attended. Two COGIC bishops eulogized her. After the funeral, Tony asked if I wanted to come live with him in St. Louis, Missouri. I called Cynthia and told her that I would be moving to St. Louis.

Chapter Twelve

IN FEBRUARY 2011, I MOVED IN WITH MY COUSIN TO LOUIS, Missouri. His apartment building was in front of a bus stop. While Tony was at work, I spent my days at the nearby public library updating and sending out resumes to hundreds of companies. I never received a response or interview from any company. I had a Doctor of Medicine degree and did not understand why no one would hire me. I met men that had multiple felonies on their record who did not have a problem finding a job. My cousin-in-law told me about a part-time job at a call center. This time, I lied about my felony conviction on the application. They hired me after hearing my voice on a mock phone solicitation. The job paid minimum wage for working a maximum of twenty hours a week.

The first couple of days went well. They seated me next to a young Black woman who appeared to be a recovering drug addict. By the end of the week, she created an embarrassing scene with me. Prior to the start of the shift, she came toward me pointing her finger, "Yawl should hear what I heard about this nigger." Then she gathered small groups of her female co-workers and led them into the lady's room. I knew it had something to do with me but could not imagine what it was since I just moved to this city. I remained composed and knew a confrontation with her would get me fired. I knew what she told them was extremely negative because the other workers and staff avoided any interaction with me. Most of the workers were felons on parole or probation, several workers had served time for murder and other serious criminal offenses.

One day, I boarded the bus to go home after my morning shift. A bearded young black man was the driver. He waved for me to come up front and said, "The police are spreading foul shit about you around town. A detective had come to our bus garage and showed the workers your picture. He told us that if we see you on our bus, quietly warn other passengers that you are a dangerous sex offender." I thanked him and sat back down. When I reached my destination on that bus one day, I exited through the back door. A shirtless young white man emerged from a crowd of white folks, pointed at me, and repeatedly screamed "There he is!"

I purchased a used pickup truck. There were two occasions after work when I noticed that someone had unlocked the passenger door of my truck. Everyone at the call center were accustomed to seeing me waiting to catch the bus. Then, unexpectedly, I am driving. They may have told the police I stole the truck. Anyway, the county police had the capacity to search my truck while I was inside on the phone. It did not take long for my suspicions to be confirmed. One afternoon, on my way home from work a county police cruiser was driving close to my tail. I was well within the speed limit and was not pulled over by the deputy. Suddenly, the cruiser swerved around me and sped off. A week later, I received an email notice from Google that my driving record was posted over the internet.

I moved into a high-rise building just blocks away from my cousin. When people glanced at me on the street, they changed directions or crossed the street. A gay couple lived in the corner home on my block. One day, they spoke, introduced themselves, and one mentioned they belonged to the neighborhood watch group. He told me to be careful because the police gave their watch organization a photo of me with my criminal profile. I now had insight into why total strangers reacted to me with fear.

I had a good relationship with Stefanie, my white building manager. She dated a county deputy sheriff. One Saturday, when I returned home from work, my next-door neighbor told me that a police S.W.A.T. team had been to my apartment. I immediately called the 911 emergency number to ask if they were looking for me. They gave the number to my local precinct. When I called, they asked about my birthday. Minutes later, an officer said that I was not wanted by them.

I called Stefanie, who told me what happened. "Yes, the police did come to your apartment several times today. The white lady in the apartment above you called the police. She claimed that you robbed and assaulted her. We reviewed the film from the lobby and outside building cameras, which showed you leaving the building early this morning and never returning. It would have been impossible to have been at her apartment at the time she claimed the robbery and assault took place. We know that you were working today. I am glad that you were not home when the police arrived. Right now, you would probably be in the county morgue. Those cameras saved your life."

I was coming out of a local grocery store when a black St. Louis police officer working security addressed me as "Doc." I told him that was my prison nickname. The officer said he had my criminal profile in his office and a bulletin about me was sent to all major retailers in the country.

I got a post office box but often received my letters and large parcels opened. I raised hell about it numerous times. The branch supervisor always claimed ignorance of the breach of my privacy. Some of my outgoing mail never reached its destination. People often complained about not receiving the mail I sent them.

I saw a commercial on television about an internet company called "Your Reputation. Com." They specialized in finding slanderous information posted online about people. I reached an answering service and left a message with my phone number. Within minutes, an attorney returned my call. He said, "Dr. Johnson, that manslaughter conviction is not what's hurting you. Have you seen that picture of you over the internet?" Then, he gave me the following URLs: Sex Offender. Com/directory/in/j/van_johnson_653503; the public record repository. Com/public-record-services-2/re; van Johnson Muncie sex offender record. Com/directory/in/van Johnson; hominy. Com.

When I logged into the "van johnson Muncie sex offender" website, the webpage displayed my prison photo and name in large font under the banner, "SEX OFFENDER...WARN YOUR NEIGHBORS, FRIENDS, and PROTECT YOUR CHILDREN." Voluntary Manslaughter was the listed offense. The following message was at the bottom of the page: Please tell a friend or relative and prevent them from becoming the next victim. So, railroading me to prison was not enough to quench the white community's thirst for revenge. That slander and defamation of my character forced a lot of Black people to finally question the integrity of the judicial system and police. Many black people thought: If they lied about the sex offense, what else did they lie about to obtain the manslaughter conviction.

Another internet company named "Internet reputation. Com" sent me several emails about the existence of four websites that had claimed I killed a child during a rape. The site "hominy. Com," got even more creative with their Libel. "Dr. Van Johnson was arrested twice for sex offenses while on parole in Muncie. He was already on Muncie's sex offender registry." A sex offense is a serious crime. If what they posted was true, it constituted a profoundly serious parole violation. I would have been immediately sent back to prison. The county prosecutor would have taken me to trial for that crime.

I called Nancy Marvin, who supervised the Muncie sex offender registry. I asked her why my name and prison photo were all over the internet as a sex offender. She denied any knowledge of the matter, saying, "When you completed parole, we took your name off all registries. It had never been placed on any sex offender registry because you did not commit that category of criminal offense." I asked if the police or prosecutor's office in Anderson was responsible for the internet post. She remained quiet and refused my request to have it removed.

So, it was obvious that the Indiana law enforcement and judicial system had weaponized the internet to kill everything about me, by any means necessary. I am just another powerless negro – or prisoner of war– trapped in a world ruled by white supremacy.

I applied for an apartment in a nearby housing complex and received a letter of rejection. Sherry, the property manager, sent me a letter explaining why they rejected my application—the manslaughter conviction and the National Sex Offender Registry. The latter was unbelievable. In the past, I made several inquiries to Sherry about my housing needs. I contacted Sherry about the rejection letter. I explained that the manslaughter conviction took place over thirty years ago and that I was never been arrested for a sex offense. Sherry responded, "Van, we do not have a problem with the manslaughter conviction. But that goddamn sex offender shit scares the hell out of people. Look, you are going to have to deal with that matter now or later."

My relatives in law enforcement said that I was in a dire situation. "Being projected as a violent sex fiend sets you up for assassination by the police, a hit man, or some irrational person seeking fanfare. You know too much, and must be silenced somehow," they opined. They suggested I draft my entire story and send it to every Black civil rights organization, black congressmen, newspapers, and magazines." I put together an information packet and sent it to every black civil rights organization, ACLU, New Yorker magazine, New York Times, and the Washington Post newspaper. None of the so-called civil rights organizations or news media responded with any interest.

I sent a letter to Mr. Matthew W. Drake, FBI Chief of Civil Rights, Criminal Investigative Division. He instructed me to send specific details with supporting documents to their field St. Louis field office. I followed his instructions but never received any feedback.

William Lacy Clay, the U.S. representative for Missouri's first district, replied that his office would open an investigation into the matter.

I returned a signed congressional release of information form, but his office never responded to inquiries about the investigation.

I was worried that the internet slander of being a sex offender would never go away because I was not receiving any feedback from the two federal investigations. When I brought the matter to the attention of a lawyer, he told me that federal and government agencies never disclose the nature of their investigations. He was correct; one day that material disappeared from the internet. I thank Congressman Clay's office and the civil rights division of the FBI.

Wm. LACY CLAY
1st District, Missouri

COMMITTEES:
FINANCIAL SERVICES
Ranking Member,
SUBCOMMITTEE ON
DOMESTIC AND INTERNATIONAL
MONETARY POLICY

OVERSIGHT AND
GOVERNMENT REFORM
Member,
SUBCOMMITTEE ON
FEDERAL WORKFORCE,
U.S. POSTAL SERVICE AND THE CENSUS

Web Site: www.lacyclay.house.gov/

Congress of the United States
House of Representatives
Washington, DC 20515-2501

2418 Rayburn House Office Building
Washington, DC 20515
(202) 225-2406
(202) 226-3717 Fax

6830 Gravois Ave.
St. Louis, MO 63116
(314) 669-9393
(314) 669-9398 Fax

Thomas F. Eagleton U.S. Court House
111 S. Tenth Street, Suite 24.344
St. Louis, MO 63102
(314) 367-1970
(314) 367-1341 Fax

October 20, 2014

Van Johnson
P.O. Box 19003
St. Louis, MO 63118

Dear Van Johnson,

Thank you for allowing me to assist with your case. Although I cannot guarantee a particular outcome, I want you to know that my staff and I will do our best to help you receive a fair and timely response to your concerns.

As my staff addresses the situation you have described, please bear in mind that they cannot force an agency to expedite your case or to act in your favor. Also, my office is not able to offer legal advice or recommend an attorney. The rules of the House of Representatives prevent me from intervening in or influencing the outcome of cases that are under the jurisdiction of any court. Finally, my office cannot intervene in matters under the jurisdiction of local or state governments.

Once your privacy release is received, my office will begin work on your case. Please understand that some cases may require a length of time to fully review. If you have any further questions, feel free to call my office at (314) 669-9393.

Sincerely,

Wm. Lacy Clay
Member of Congress

The medical board of Indiana gave permission to reapply for licensure. However, the length of time that I had not practiced medicine, and the false stigmatization "Sex Offender" foreclosed any chance of regaining licensure anywhere. The white supremacists of Indiana knew that a sex offender label insured total ex-communicated from society.

I contacted Sonja to get an update on her life. She had a sense of humor. "Did you drop the soap?" She married a real screwball. He called and threatened me for talking to her. Sonja called the next day to say it was okay to call. I did not understand why she denied being married. She was not happy because he drank and beat on her. I played it cool and did not call again.

In 2014, I did not have a car and had to get up early in the morning to take public transportation to work. About 2:00 a.m., Sonya called and disrupted my sleep. She told me that they had diagnosed her with stage four breast cancer. Both breast and the upper lobe of her right lung had to be surgically removed. Her life was statistically ending with that type of diagnosis. Of the surgeries, she had radiation and chemotherapy. A nurse came every two weeks to start an IV line and deliver the chemo in her veins. I would call her every day after my shift at 12:30 p.m. We'd talk until she was too weak to talk anymore. She eventually recovered and is doing well today.

Rosie successfully obtained a doctorate degree and is the director of a juvenile correctional facility in Jackson, Mississippi.

I found out from several prisoners from Anderson that Dr. Ramaswamy, the Indian doctor, who tried to get me involved in his practice, had signed a plea agreement with federal prosecutors. No one knew the details of his prison sentence. But he did go to the big house(prison) as well. St. John's Hospital took over his million dollar-a-year psychiatry practice. The White power structure of Anderson had successfully eliminated the only two non-white psychiatrists in that town.

The injustice I received in this country's white supremacy judicial system received national and international attention from prominent Black and white columnists, scholars, and civil rights leaders.

Epilogue

IF A BLACK MAN IS ACCUSED OF DOING ANY HARM TO A white person, all that is needed for a conviction is a jury of mostly white people. That is the threshold, not the evidence, as one would think. After my release from prison, why would they place my prison photo over the internet as a Sex Offender? People came to the conclusion that they lied on me to obtain the manslaughter conviction, as well. The ordeal I experienced was the failed result of attempted insurance fraud through murder.

Addendum

Title

         Title of Work: Framed and Profiled; the Legal Lynching of a black Psychiatrist

Completion/Publication

        Year of Completion: 2013

Author

      ■   Author: Van Johnson

    Author Created: text

       Citizen of: United States

       Year Born: 1954

Copyright claimant

    Copyright Claimant: Van Johnson

                P O Box 19003, saint louis, MO, 63118, United States

Certification

          Name: van johnson

           Date: July 23, 2013

IN THE
CIRCUIT COURT OF MADISON COUNTY
STATE OF INDIANA

VAN JOHNSON, MD Petitioner,	)))
Prison No. 923123	) Cause No. **48C01-9006-CF-057**
STATE OF INDIANA, Respondent.	)))

AMENDED PRETITION FOR POST CONVICTION RELIEF

COMES NOW, Petitioner, Van Johnson, M.D. ("Dr. Johnson"), *pro-se* pursuant to Indiana Post-Conviction Rule 1, (4)(C), and amends his *pro se* Petition For Post Conviction Relief.

Specification 8 is amended to list the ground for vacating Dr. Johnson's conviction as follows:

> **8(a) Dr. Johnson's right to due process, due course of law, the effective assistance of counsel, and equal protection under the Fifth, Sixth, and Fourteenth Amendment of the United States Constitution, and Article One § Twelve, Thirteen and Twenty-three of the Indiana Constitution were violated when <u>appellate counsel failed to raise the issue that the trial court compelled the defendant to appear at trial in jail clothing.</u>**

8(b) Dr. Johnson's right to due process, due course of law, the effective assistance of counsel, and equal protection under the Fifth, Sixth, and Fourteenth Amendment of the United States Constitution, and Article One § Twelve, Thirteen and Twenty-three of the Indiana Constitution were violated when appellate counsel failed inadequately presented the issue that trial court "Erred" in denying defense request for mistrial.

8(c) Dr. Johnson's right to due process, due course of law, the effective assistance of counsel, and equal protection under the Fifth, Sixth, and Fourteenth Amendment of the United States Constitution, and Article One § Twelve, Thirteen and Twenty-three of the Indiana Constitution were violated when appellate counsel failed to raise the issue of trial counsel ineffectiveness for failure to tender jury instructions on Reckless Homicide.

8(d) Dr. Johnson's right to due process, due course of law, the effective assistance of counsel, and equal protection under the Fifth, Sixth, and Fourteenth Amendment of the United States Constitution, and Article One § Twelve, Thirteen and Twenty-three of the Indiana Constitution were violated when the defendant was denied a fair trial when the State Introduced evidence at trial that had been altered.

Specification 9 is amended to state the facts and circumstances to support the grounds listed in specification 8.

9(a) Appellate counsel's failure to raise the Issue that Trial Court Erred in compelling defendant to appear before jury in Jail Clothing was constitutionally deficient performance because he omitted a Dead-Bang Winner.

This term is not defined by the courts but refers to an issue appellate counsel failed to raise which "was obvious from the record, and must have leaped out upon even a casual reading of the transcript," and which would have resulted in a reversal of conviction on direct appeal. See *Page v. U.S.* 884 F.2d 300 (C.A.7 (Wis) 1989); *U.S. v. Cook*, 45 F.3d 388 (10th Cir. 1995); *Banks v. Reynolds*, 54 F.3d 1508 (10th Cir. 1995);

2

Matire v. Wainwright, 811 F.2d at 1439 (C.A. (Fla.) 1987). By omitting an issue under these circumstances counsel's performance is "<u>objectively</u>" deficient because the omitted issue is obvious from the trial record. *Matire v. Wainwright*, 811 F.2d 1430, 1438 (11th Cir. 1987).

The standard for <u>ineffective assistance</u> is the same for trial and appellate counsel *Peoples v. Bowen*, 791 F.2d 861 (11th Cir) denied U.S. 107 S. Ct. 597, 93 L.Ed. 2d 597 (1986). However to make a successful claim of ineffective assistance of counsel a defendant must show that his counsel's performance was deficient and that the deficient performance prejudiced his defense. *Strickland v. Washington*, 466 U.S. 668, 687; 104 S. Ct. 2052, 2064; 80 L.Ed. 2d 674 (1984).

Issues that were or could have been raised on direct appeal are not available for review in Post-Conviction proceedings. *Weatherford v. State*, 619 N.E.2d 915, 917 (Ind. 1993) (citing *Brown v. State*, 261 Ind. 619, 308 N.E. 2d 699 (1974).

A defendant can't raise claims that were not presented on Direct Appeal unless he can show cause-and-prejudice resulting from the error. A defendant may establish cause for his procedural default by showing that he received ineffective assistance of counsel in violation of the Sixth Amendment. *Murray v. Carrier*, 477 U.S. 478, 488, 91 L.Ed.2d 397, 106 S.Ct. 2639 (1986); *Weatherford v. State*, 619 N.E.2d 915, 917 (Ind. 1993).

The omitted issue in this case involves the Trial Court compelling Dr. Johnson to appear at trial in Jail Clothing. This appearance before the venire jury unconstitutionally infringed upon his due process right to be presumed innocent until proven guilty under Fourteenth Amendment. *Hernandez v. Beto*, 443 F.2d 634 (5th Cir., 1971), Cert. Denied

3

404 U.S. 897, 92 S. Ct. 201, 30 L.Ed.2d 174 (1971); *Bentley v. Crist*, 469 F.2d 854 (9th Cir. 1972).

This case has many similarities to *Gaito v. Brierley*, 485 F.2d 86, (C.A.3 (PA.) 1973). Both cases involve re-trials following reversal of conviction in respective state courts. Both defendants were compelled to appear before a Venire jury in jail clothing, and were denied "motion" for mistrial at voir dire.

In *Gaito v. Brierley, Supra*, the United States court of Appeal, 3rd circuit (PA) reversed *Gaito's* conviction on the grounds that his right to Due Process were infringed because he was compelled to appear before the venire jury in prison clothing.

Chronology of how trial Court compelled Petitioner to appear before Venire Jury in Jail Clothing:

The Indiana Supreme Court reversed defendant's conviction for voluntary manslaughter on September 15, 1995. On January 11, 1996, the Madison County Circuit Court issued an order for the Sheriff to transport the defendant from the Indiana State Prison to the Madison County detention Center on 1-15-96 (R.p. 263).

The defendant was given a bail of 75,000,00 cash bond which he couldn't afford. (R.p. 468) . He requested to be released on his own recognizance, this was also denied. (R.p. 449). The defendant remained in the County Jail from January 1996 to June 7, 1996 when his second trial commenced. (R.p.508).

On 3-29-96, defense trial counsel filed a motion entitled: **"Notice of Indigence and request for expenses for payment of necessary Expenses and Costs for the defense of the defendant."** This motion asked the court for $600.00 to purchase a suit for the defendant to wear at trial; it also reminded the court of the defendant's indigent

4

status, and put the court on notice that the "defendant did not desire to be tried in such Jail Clothing, and He objected to being tried in Jail Clothing, (R.p. 312).

At a Pre-trial conference held on 4-1-96 to discuss the above motion, the trial Judge stated that he would not allow $600.00 for a suit. Defense counsel said that he would accept a lesser amount or whatever the court would allow. e.g. defense counsel stated:

> "Judge, how about I just get Mr. Johnson one pair of pants, 2 shirts, and a Jacket?" The Prosecutor joined the discussion and said it was absurd to purchase clothing for him (defendant) when they (court) don't do it for other defendants. The trial Judge then said the motion was denied, and that he would not release any funds for defendant's clothing. (R.p.470).

There is no standard related to how much a court should allow for clothing. A defense attorney motions the court concerning a need and its at the courts discretion to release whatever amount it feels necessary. The amount of money requested in this instance was not unreasonable because prior to the commencement of the first trial in May 1992, a similar motion was filed by defense counsel and the same Judge released $750.00 for clothing (R.p. 188-89).

The Court acknowledged Dr. Johnson's objection to being tried in jail clothes by this declaration:

> Trial Judge, "He cannot be allowed in court at [trial] in those jail clothes." I am obligated to make sure you don't appear at trial in jail clothes (R.p. 467-470).

At the conclusion of this pre-trial conference, the court stated that if the defendant didn't have any clothes for trial by 5-29-96, the court would hold a special session to address the issue to purchase clothing. (R.p. 475). The defendant never got clothing for trial because there was no meeting by the court on 5-29-96.

5

When Sheriff Deputies brought Dr. Johnson to court at the commencement of his trial on 6-7-96 in jail clothing the Court contravened the law by <u>compelling</u> him to be there in such clothing. This violated the defendant's right to due process and equal protection of the law under the fourteenth amendment as expressed in *Estelle v. Williams*, S.Ct. **1691, 425 U.S. 501, (U.S.Tex. 1976)**

Dr. Johnson had a constitutional right to a 'Presumption of Innocence' because the offense for which was being re-tried, occurred while he was a practicing medical Doctor/Psychiatrist in civilian life, unlike the appellant in *U.S. ex rel. Stahl v. Henderson* **472 F.2d 556 (C.A.S.), cert. Denied, 411 U.S. 971, 93 S.Ct. 2166, 36 L.Ed.2d 694 (1973).**

This clothing issue was the most dominant, pervasive theme throughout the pre-trial conferences and this issue should have been raised on direct appeal as a Free-Standing Constitutional issue. This issue is clearly the strongest of all the ones presented on direct appeal. *Gray v. Greer*, **800 F.2d 644, 646 (7th Cirt. 1986).**

At the commencement of trial on 6-7-96 <u>the Petitioner was brought into the court by Sheriff Deputies in Jail House Clothing</u>. When he arrived the jury was already seated. Judge Spencer immediately brought the court to session and asked defense counsel if he had anything to say. Trial counsel asked the defendant to stand and made an "Exhibit" of his appearance i.e. he described his client as wearing a Blue Shirt and pants normally worn by inmates at county jail (R.p. 509). The defendant motioned the Court for a mistrial. Trial Judge asked why? Defendant reminded court that he previously objected to being tried in jail clothing and that he was being prejudiced in the eyes of the jury. The judge denied the motion for mistrial: (after review of the trial transcripts, this motion for mistrial

6

was illegally expunged from the record. **(See Affidavit to reaffirm motion for mistrial made by Petitioner at Voir Dire)**. The trial court erred in denying this motion for mistrial at Voir Dire.

At Voir Dire, defense counsel Montague Oliver Jr. Challenged venire juror Mr. Claypool regarding his attitude towards Dr. Johnson:

> Attorney Oliver - The fact that they've brought him in here and charged him with a crime, does that mean anything to you? Juror Mr. Claypool: **"I guess it implies [guilt] that He[]s in jail."** (Voir Dire Transcript, State of Indiana v. Van Johnson Cause no. 48C01-9006-CF-057, Pg. 193).

There was no curative response from the court following this statement by Mr. Claypool, and he sat on the final Jury panel that convicted Dr. Johnson in approximately 20 minutes (R.p. 1265). It's obvious that Dr. Johnson's appearance in jail clothing compromised his Presumption of Innocence.

When the Court compelled the Defendant to appear before the Venire Jury in jail clothing, it was not harmless error beyond a reasonable doubt. **Chapman v. California, 386 U.S.18,17 L.Ed.2d 705, 87 S.Ct. 824 (1967).**

If appellate counsel had raised the issue that Trial court Erred in compelling the defendant to appear at trial in jail clothing, the appellate court would have been mandated by law to reverse the conviction. Moreover, Appellate counsel's performance in regard to this issue was deficient and prejudiced defendant by omitting an obvious constitutional claim.

> **9(b) Appellate counsel wrote in his "Statement of the Issues" in the Brief of Appellant Blue Book, that the trial court erred when it denied the defense motion for mistrial.**

7

DR. VAN JOHNSON, M.D.

However, when this issue was "BRIEFED," counsel simply wrote that a motion for mistrial was made and denied without claiming error; provided no argument or citation to support any such claim. **As a result of this deficient performance the appellate court ruled, Issue was "Waived" under Ind. Appellate Rule 8.3 (A)(7) see Memorandum decision of the Court of Appeals of Indiana pg. 3. (February 24, 1998 Indiana Court of Appeal 48A02-9610-CR-664).**

In *Bieghler v. State*, 690 N.E.2d 188, (Ind. 1997), 3 different categories of appellate ineffectiveness is identified. In this case the issue coincides with the Third category: appellate counsel raised a particular issue but its Presentation was inadequate in some way. Though technically raised, is deemed waived for failure to present cogent argument and/or cite authority, or facts in the record supporting the claim. *Goliday v. State*, 526 N.E.2d 1174, 1175 (Ind. 1988); *Ashford v. State*, 464 N.E. 2d 1298, 1302 (Ind. 1984).

In the instant case, appellate counsel wrote in his "statement of the issues" that the Trial Court "Erred" in denying defense request for Mistrial, but failed to state whether the Court Erred, in his Brief of this issue. See Brief of Appellant Blue Book (Raised under Prosecutorial misconduct, Issue No. 3).

Appellate counsel's inadequate presentation of this issue caused "Waiver" of claim in appellate court. We must now examine the waived issue for merit.

The Prosecutor on closing argument was refuting defense claim that shooting was an accident by alleging that defendant was guilty of violating **IC-35-47-4-3** for pointing the Firearm at the decedent. Defense moved for a mistrial which the court denied (R.p. 1225-

8

26). Defense counsel reminded the court that defendant had not been charged with that crime.

This was clearly Reversible error in denying the defense motion for mistrial. Due Process requires that a defendant be given clear notice of the charges against which the state summons him to defend. **Ind. Const. 1§ 13;** *Blackburn v. State* **(1973), 260 Ind. 5, 11, 291 N.E.2d 686, 690, appeal dismissed;** *Blackburn v. Indiana,* **412 U.S. 925, 93 S.Ct. 2755, 37 L.Ed.2d 152.**

The prosecutor then proceeded to tell the Jury that the elements of his charge is that 'he knowingly or intentionally killed, and it is not charged as an accident, reckless anything else, this . . . He knew what he was doing." (R.p. 1197). It is clear that the state sought only to charge defendant with Voluntary Manslaughter. See *Sills v. State* **(1984), Ind. 463 N.E.2d 228, 235, Reh. Denied (Citing** *Jones v. State* **(1982), Ind. 438 N.E.2d 972).**

In a homicide case no mention or consideration should be given to non-homicide lesser offenses. *Swafford v. State* **(1981), Ind. 421 N.E.2d 596. IC 35-47-4-3** is pointing a firearm. This and Criminal Recklessness require Knowingly or intentionally pointing a firearm at another person, and was the same offense for double jeopardy purposes.

So when the prosecutor said the defendant violated **IC 35-47-4-3** in the commission of the crime, he alluded to an offense that should not have been mentioned or considered because this case involved a homicide. The defendant's right to due process was clearly violated and the state should have granted defendant's request for a mistrial.

9

Appellate counsel rendered ineffective assistance for inadequate presentation in that he failed to mention in his "Brief" of this Issue, Whether the Court "Erred in denying the defense request for mistrial, nor did he give argument or any citation in support of such claim. If counsel had wrote that the court "Erred" in denying mistrial with supporting argument and citation, the appellate court would have reversed conviction because of the obvious Due Process Violation.

> 9(c) Appellate Counsel's failure to raise Issue on Direct Appeal concerning trial counsel's failure to tender Reckless Homicide Instructions was deficient performance which resulted in "Waiver of a meritorious claim.

The review of ineffective assistance of appellate counsel uses that same standard applicable to claims of trial counsel's ineffectiveness. *Ben-Yisrayl v. State*, 729 N.E.2d 102, 106 (Ind. 2000). The defendant must show that appellate counsel was deficient in his performance and that the deficiency resulted in prejudice. Ineffective assistance claims at the appellate level of proceedings generally fall into three basic categories: 1) denial of access to an appeal; 2) Waiver of Issues; and 3) Failure to present issues well. *Bieghler v. State*, 690 N.E.2d 188, 193-95 (Ind. 1997). The defendant (appellant) is basing appellate counsel's error on the second category – waiver of Issue.

In *Timberlake v. State*, 753 N.E.2d 591, 605 (Ind. 2001)(quoting Bieghler, 690 N.E.2d at 194), Cert. Denied, 537 U.S. 839, 154 L.Ed.2d 61, 123 S.Ct. 162 (2002). The courts employ a two-part test to evaluate "waiver of Issues" claims: 1) Whether the unraised issue(s) are significant and obvious from the face of the record. 2) Whether the unraised issues are "clearly stronger" than the raised issues. *Gray v. Greer*, 800 F.2d 644 (7th Cir. 1985).

10

The significant, and strongest **unraised** issue in this case is whether trial counsel rendered deficient performance for failure to tender jury instructions on Reckless Homicide, the inherently lesser-included offense of Voluntary Manslaughter.

Dr. Van Johnson was charged by information of the crime of Voluntary Manslaughter **IC-35-42-1-3**, which is a person who knowingly or intentionally kills another human being, while acting under sudden heat .

~Reckless Homicide **IC 35-42-1-5**, A person who recklessly kills another human being commits reckless homicide, a class C felony.

Reckless Homicide is an inherently included offense of Voluntary Manslaughter in that only distinguishing feature between two offenses is lesser culpability required to establish Reckless Homicide. *Ford v. State*, **439 N.E.2d 648, (Ind. App. 1982).**

The state cannot draft an information that forecloses an instruction on an inherently lesser-included offense of crime charged, the state may by proper drafting of charging instrument,   avoid charging factually included lesser-offense of crime charged. *Aschliman v. State* **(1992), Ind, 589 N.E.2d 1160, 1161.**

The law governing lesser-included offenses were clarified in *Wright v. State*, **658 N.E.2d 563 (Ind. 1995).** There is a three-part test that trial courts should perform when called upon by a party to instruct a jury on a lesser-included offense of the crime charged. Only the third part of this applies to the case at bar: If a trial court has determined that a lesser-included offense is either inherently or factually included in the crime charged, it must look at the evidence presented in the case by both parties to determine if there is a serious evidentiary dispute about the element or elements distinguishing the greater from the lesser offense and if, in view of this dispute, a jury could conclude that the lesser

11

offense was committed but not the greater. It is reversible error for a trial court not to give an instruction when requested, on the inherently or factually included lesser offense when there is such an evidentiary dispute.

There is a serious evidentiary dispute produced by evidence from both parties in this case: 1) After his arrest defendant told police "I didn't mean to kill the guy" (R.p. 1242) 2) During closing arguments, the state told the jury that defendant's conduct was "reckless" in the commission of the crime; and that he violated **I.C. 35-47-4-3** (by Pointing a firearm, a Class D Felony – R.p. 1225), and 3) Trial counsel argued that the state did not prove that the defendant knowingly killed while under sudden heart (R.p. 1242). The evidentiary dispute is whether the defendant knowingly or recklessly killed (i.e. the *mens rea* of the defendant).

The trial court would have instructed jury on Reckless Homicide if trial counsel had tendered such instruction.

Voluntary Manslaughter statute, when coupled with Criminal Recklessness statute is generally applied to individuals who engage in random dangerous conduct which is not necessarily directed at another, but which results in foreseeable death of another. *Young v. State* **(Ind. 1998), 699 N.E.2d 252.**

To Warrant a jury finding of Reckless Homicide, there must be a demonstration that the defendant acted recklessly! If there was a suggestion of the existence of requisite reckless conduct, it creates a serious evidentiary dispute that would enable a jury to conclude that defendant did not commit Voluntary Manslaughter (Murder mitigated by presence of sudden heat) but instead committed Reckless Homicide. *Ellis v. State,* **(Ind. 2000), 736 N.E.2d 731.**

12

In the instant case, the state in refuting the defense of accident told jury,

"How much more reckless can you be than to meet somebody at your front door with a shotgun aimed at them and ready to fire with the safety off? How much more reckless could you be? (R.p. 1225).

Trial Counsel's failure to tender the jury instructions for Reckless Homicide was constitutionally deficient performance in light of a serious evidentiary dispute which left the jury to speculate on a third factual situation. *Hash v. State,* **(1972) 258 Ind. 692, 284 N.E.2d 770**.

Without the instruction on the lesser included offense, the charge to the jury was misleading in presenting the jury only with the options of convicting defendant of an intentional killing or acquitting him. *Sharkey v. State,* **672 N.E.2d 937, (Ind. App. 1996)**, criticized, *Fisher v. State,* **785 N.E.2d 320 (Ind. App. 2003)**; *Roark v. State,* **573 N.E.2d 881, 883 (Ind. 1991).** ~~get S. ce Decision~~

An instruction on <u>self-defense</u> was given in this case over defense Counsel objection (R.p. 1172-1173). The defense didn't hinge on self-defense, and trial Counsel's failure to tender jury instruction on the lesser included offense was not a matter of strategy. *Sarwacinski v. State,* **564 N.E.2d 950 (Ind. Ct. App. 1991).**

Trial Counsel based his defense on lack of intent, i.e. the defense of accident and Voluntary Intoxication. Although jury rejected both defense, if instructions on Reckless Homicide were given, the jury could have returned a conviction of Reckless Homicide instead of Voluntary Manslaughter depending on how it weighed and credited all of the evidence.

As such, trial Counsel's failure to tender Final Jury instruction for Reckless Homicide, the lesser- included offense of Voluntary Manslaughter was reversible error.

13

Appellate counsel's failure to present this claim on Direct Appeal amounted to ineffective assistance.

9(d) Altered evidence introduced at trial was crime scene photographs of decedent's attire.

This evidence was originally submitted to the court as State's Exhibit 15.19, and 20. Found in Record of Proceedings (**48A02-CR-166/48S02-9503-CR-345**) Volume 9 of 18; pages 2190, 2191, 2192, respectively. Prosecutor William Lawler was granted leave of court to submit these exhibits without objections from Defense Counsel. Mr. Tom Broderick, Jr. (R.p. 2189) at trial.

This crime scene pictorial evidence was shown to two juries and depicted decedent in white gym shoes, blue jeans, light-colored shirt and a *Herald-Bulletin Newspaper* next to the body in the living room.

I, the Petitioner, was the only eyewitness to circumstances of the shooting. After the decedent was brought into the living room under bright lights, I saw his complete attire which consisted of brown cowboy boots, blue jeans, light-colored shirt, and a large, blue plaid, winter overcoat that had an eggshell colored, billowy wool lining. At the time, I didn't search him for weapons or his identification. (See Affidavit concerning attire of Decedent on the night of shooting June 10, 1990).

It's obvious to me that after my arrest and transport to the police station, someone switched the decedent's cowboy boots to white gym shoes, removed his large winter coat, and placed a copy of the Anderson *Herald-Bulletin Newspaper* next to his body. I was not home when police photographed, filmed, or processed the scene for evidence.

14

Prosecutor Bill Lawler and decedent's wife were in my home after I was taken to the police station.

In allowing these unauthenticated pictorial images of the decedent to be presented as evidence to a jury, the court bypassed its three requirements for admission of photographs: 1) adequate foundation: this requires the testimony of a witness who can state that the photographic evidence is true and accurate representation of things it is intended to depict. *Boone v. State*, (1978) Ind., 371 N.E.2d 208. 2) Relevancy; A photograph must meet the usual relevancy standard. (i.e., it must tend to prove or disprove a material fact.) *Smith v. Crouse-Hinds Company* (1978) Ind. App. 373 N.E.2d 923. In applying this standard to photographic evidence, courts ask whether a witness would be permitted to testify as to the subject matter portrayed in the photograph. *Simpson v. State*, (1978) Ind. , 381 N.E.2d 1229, 30). Photographs in some cases are required to aid Jurors understanding of other evidence. *Whitfield v. State* (1977) 266 Ind. 629, 366 N.E.2d 173; *McPherson v. State*, (1978) Ind. App. 383 N.E.2d 403. Whether this is truly a requirement for the admission of photographs in Indiana is not totally clear. Some cases seem to elevate it to the level of a requirement, *McPherson (supra)*, while other merely recite it as a part of the relevancy test *Whitfield (supra)*.

The Petitioner was the only witness to the shooting incident and could have testified to the authenticity of the pictorial evidence. He was never shown nor consulted about the pictorial evidence (**Attorney Patrick E. Chavis, III.**, stated that every time he asked for state's evidence against his client, he was always told that "Star China" had not processed the photo/film yet).

15

Petitioner had never seen state pictorial evidence until review of trial proceedings in preparation for post-conviction relief petition.

Photograph/film tend to have great probative weight, and should not be admitted unless the court is convinced of their competency and authenticity to a relative certainty. If admitted as substantive evidence, proof is required that the evidence depicted by the photographs has not been altered in any significant respect. See **Bergen v. State (Ind. App. 4 Dist. 1979).**

The decedent's attire was altered because the State knew that no rational person on a jury would believe that a man wearing a large winter overcoat in June came to a doctor's luxury apartment late on a Sunday night to collect a two-dollar newspaper debt. A *Herald-Bulletin Newspaper* was placed next to the body. This visually insinuates the State's claim that decedent came to Dr. Johnson's home "solely" for the purpose of collecting a newspaper debt..

If the pictorial evidence had not been altered, a jury would have acquited Dr. Johnson of criminal liability. The jury would have believed that Dr. Johnson indeed feared for his life upon seeing a man in a huge winter coat standing in front of various windows. The winter coat would have been viewed as some type of camouflage to hide his identity, conceal a weapon, but nevertheless, threatening. Being in front of various windows means he left numerous footprints in the garden soil. Switching his cowboy boots to gym shoes would hide that forensic evidence of his presence outside of bedrooms; and would alter the trajectory of shot ballistics. Also, to remove the winter coat and place gym shoes on him gave him a seasonal-appropriate, non-threatening appearance. All of the State witnesses claim that on the night of the shooting, it was a warm summer night.

16

192

Lastly, a police conspiracy to "frame" the petitioner cannot be ruled out: On June 5, 1990, a state police undercover officer named Vera Dupree came to the home of Dr. Johnson and told him that a "hit" had been placed on his life in that county and that off-duty Anderson police in conjunction with several sheriff deputies would be part of the "hit team." They were supposed to stage Dr. Johnson in a car crash on his way to Chicago. She informed him that his medical clinic office phone was illegally bugged. This state police agent also said that the "hit" was initiated by a corporate entity in Anderson. She said the defendant knew the parties involved because of a ongoing corporate dispute. That corporate dispute involved the St. John's Corporation who held a $480, 000 dollar John Handcock life insurance policy on the defendant's life. If the defendant somehow died within one year of practice there, the hospital would receive this pay-out since they were the beneficiary.

St. John's Hospital security force is predominated by retired Anderson police. This hospital corporation has direct influence on the police in that town and it is possible that the decedent may have been in collusion with the police and/ or entities of St. John's Corporation in Anderson. This can't be ruled out.

The State in this cause simply "Hoodwinked" the court in obtaining a conviction from fraudulent evidence.

The state knew it had no true criminal evidence against defendant, so the evidence was altered to project a criminal image by persuading the jury that he killed an innocent non-threatening individual who was doing a routine chore. The state's theory coupled with the altered evidence, made Dr. Johnson's statement to police seem like a hastily

17

DR. VAN JOHNSON, M.D.

made up lie. That, the defendant was covering up a cold-blooded murder without provocation.

This conviction must be vacated on the grounds that petitioner never received a fair trial because the state violated his right to Due Process under the Fifth and Fourteenth Amendments when it showed the jury Altered Attire of Decedent in crime scene photos and film. Additionally, evidence was "Planted" in the form of a newspaper placed next to decedent's body. These acts of Prosecutorial Misconduct were not "Harmless Error"!

Special limitations on harmless error are essential to the fundamental fairness guaranteed by the Due Process clauses of the Fifth and Fourteenth Amendments. Certain types of official misconduct require reversal simply because society cannot tolerate giving final effect to a judgment tainted with such

intentional misconduct. *E.G. Berger v. United States*, **295 US 78,79 L.Ed 1314, 55 S.Ct. 629 (Prosecutorial Misconduct).**

CONCLUSION

For all the foregoing reasons, the Petitioner, Dr. Van Johnson, above named, proceeding *pro se*, respectfully requests the Court to reverse, vacate, and/or remand the judgment of this Court, for proceedings that are consistent with the decisions herein, laws of the United States and/or Indiana Law and for all other relief that is just, proper,

18

African doctor railroaded

ANDERSON, IND.—Dr. Van Johnson, an African doctor who has struggled tirelessly to provide medical care to our oppressed and exploited community, has come under vicious assault by the lawless colonial white power system of Anderson, Indiana.

Brother Johnson was charged with shooting a member of the KKK, James Wagner, who invaded his home. After being railroaded through the colonial judicial system, Brother Johnson was convicted of voluntary manslaughter and sentenced to 40 years in prison.

Although friends repeatedly told Johnson that members of the medical profession wanted "to do him harm" and that the Anderson Police Department and the KKK were watching him, the court refused to hear their testimony.

A storm on June 19, 1992 during jury deliberations laid grounds for a mistrial. Attorney Thomas Broderick Jr. stated that, "At the time of the thunder storm, there was a lot of confusion among the jurors. You could hear the emergency sirens and the police sirens in the background. Lights in the courthouse went off, and the alarms sounded."

Attorney Broderick went on to say that "eventually the jurors were led to the basement. Before that the spectators and Mr. Wagner's family were all in the same room talking together."

African people in Anderson and all over Indiana and Illinois are struggling to free Dr. Van Johnson, a crusader in the struggle to liberate our people from lives of disease, poor health, and sickness due to the miserable conditions of colonialism.

For more information about how you can help free Dr. Van Johnson write to:

Dr. Van Johnson Defense Committee

P.O. Box 53325
Chicago, IL 60601

Or call Minister Tele E'mani at (312)522-4318 or (312)726-8426 ∎

*The Burning Spear
Chicago, Ill.*

DR. VAN JOHNSON, M.D.

Page 1 of 1

National Church Residences
EXCELLENCE THAT TRANSFORMS LIVES

Alexian Court
2636 Chippewa
St. Louis, MO 63118

Jan 7, 2016

Van R. Johnson
4249 Michigan ST, Apt #701
St Louis, MO 63111

Dear Van R. Johnson:

Thank you for your recent application. We regret that we are unable to approve your request.

Your application was processed by a scoring system that assigns a grade using the various items we consider in evaluating an application. The information you provided for your application did not meet our criteria for approval at this time. We are hereby informing you of certain information pursuant to the Fair Credit Reporting Act, as amended by the Consumer Credit Reporting Reform Act of 1996.

Our decision was based on one or more of the following reason(s):

- No Credit Experience
- Criminal History Does Not Meet Property Requirements
- National Sex Offender History Does Not Meet Property Requirements

Your credit report was obtained from the following credit reporting agency/ies:

RentGrow, Inc. dba Yardi Resident Screening
307 Waverley Oaks Rd, STE 301
Waltham, MA 02452
Phone: 800-736-8476 x2
www.yardi.com/yrs

The information that was provided to us may have influenced our decision, but the credit reporting agency/ies did not make the decision, and are not able to explain why it was made.

If you have been rejected for reason(s) related to the information provided in your credit report(s), you have the right to obtain a free copy of your credit report, within sixty days of the date you receive this letter, from the consumer credit reporting agency/ies which have been identified in this notice.

You have the right to dispute inaccurate information by directly conveying to the consumer credit reporting agency that you dispute the accuracy of information in your file. The agency must then, within a reasonable time period, reinvestigate and modify or remove inaccurate information. The consumer credit reporting agency may not charge a fee for this service. If reinvestigation does not resolve the dispute to your satisfaction, you may send a statement to the consumer credit reporting agency, to be kept in your file, explaining why you think the record is inaccurate. The consumer credit reporting agency must include your statement about the disputed information, or a clear and accurate codification or summary thereof, in a report it issues about you.

If reason(s) are not given in this notice for why you have been rejected, you have the right to obtain disclosure of the nature of the information that was relied upon by making a written request to us within 60 days of receiving this letter.

If you have been rejected due to criminal and/or eviction history, you may contact Yardi Resident Screening at 1-800-736-8476, option 2 or go to http://www.yardi.com/yrs for assistance.

You may have additional rights under the credit reporting or consumer protection laws of your state. For further information, you can contact your state or local consumer protection agency or your state attorney general's office.

Thank you again for your interest.

Sincerely,

Sherry Snodgrass

Property Manager

Alexian Court Apartments

2636 Chippewa St   Saint Louis, MO 63118   Phone: (314)-771-5604 Fax: (314)-771-7629   TDD: 614.442.4390 www.nationalchurchresidences.org

National Church Residences does not discriminate in any fashion based upon a person's race, color, sex, national origin, handicap status, religion, marital or familial status, source of income, sexual orientation, gender identity, or disability. National Church Residences does not discriminate based upon age for any reason, excluding HUD program/project requirements.

https://login.yardiresidentscreening.com/ts2/findApp/letters/letter.jsp   1/7/2016

196

Doctor on trial denied right to attend funeral

3/19/92
Defender

by Justin Blum

A psychiatrist awaiting trial in an allegedly racially-motivated fatal shooting in Indiana was denied an opportunity to attend his father's funeral in Chicago earlier this week because county sheriff officials said they could not afford to transport him.

In a telephone interview from the holding center, Dr. Van Johnson, 37, who has been held without bond for nearly two years in Anderson, Ind., said he was "devastated" by not being able to attend his father's funeral or to even view the body at the funeral home.

He maintained that other inmates in the facility, including many repeat offenders with a history of violent crimes, had been granted emergency leave to visit a sick relative or a funeral of a loved one, Johnson said.

Johnson's lawyer, Montague Oliver Jr., said the Madison sheriff's office said a manpower shortage prevented them from transporting him to the funeral.

Johnson, who is Black, is accused in the June 1990 murder of James Wagner, a white man who authorities claimed was attempting to collect money from Johnson for newspapers the victim's son had delivered.

The psychiatrist, however, said the shooting occurred accidentally

after he went to his door, with gun in hand, to investigate why the victim allegedly was running from window-to-window at 10 p.m. on a Sunday.

Johnson claimed harassment and death threats he had received in the predominantly white community led him to bring a gun to the door.

Oliver said he asked Madison County, Ind., Circuit Court Judge Frederick Spencer last Friday to order the Sheriff's Office to transport him to Chicago for the funeral of his father, Jonathan Melvin Ivy.

But after the judge consulted Sheriff Scott Mellinger, he ruled that Johnson could not be transported unless he was willing to pay the travel expenses for two escorting officers. But Johnson could not afford to pay, according to Oliver, because the suspect's assets reportedly have been frozen by the court.

197

IN THE

CIRCUIT COURT OF MADISON COUNTY

STATE OF INDIANA

VAN JOHNSON, MD Petitioner,	)	
	)	
	)	
Prison No. 923123	)	Cause No. **48C01-9006-CF-057**
	)	
STATE OF INDIANA,	)	
Respondent.	)	

AMENDED PETITION FOR POST-CONVICTION RELIEF

COMES NOW, Petitioner, Van Johnson, M.D., ("Dr. Johnson"), *Pro se,* pursuant to Indiana Post-Conviction Rule 1, (4) (C), and amends his Petition for Post-Conviction Relief.

Specification 8 is amended to list the grounds for vacating Dr. Johnson's conviction:

8(a) Dr. Johnson's right to due process, due course of law, the effective assistance of counsel, and equal protection under the Fifth, Sixth and Fourteenth Amendments of the United States Constitution, and Article One, Section Twelve, Thirteen and twenty-Three of the Indiana Constitution were violated when <u>appellate counsel failed to raise the issue that the trial court compelled the defendant to appear at trial in jail clothing.</u>

CERTIFICATE OF FINAL DISCHARGE
State Form 49 (R4 / 7-07)
INDIANA PAROLE BOARD

Name (last, first, middle initial)			Department of Correction number
JOHNSON, VAN			923123

Expiration date of sentence (month, day, year)	Expiration date of parole period (month, day, year)	Name of committing court
06/21/2010	06/21/2010	MADISON CIRCUIT 1

Crime	Cause number	Count
VOLUNTARY MANSLAUGHTER	48C01-9006-CF-057	001

This document certifies that the above named person has been granted a Final Discharge from his/her commitment to the Indiana Department of Correction under the above Cause number and Count pursuant to:

☐ IC 35-50-6-1 based upon the maximum expiration of his/her sentence or completion of the maximum parole period; or,

☑ IC 11-13-3-5 following a review of his/her parole records by the Indiana Parole Board.

Any and all obligations to the State of Indiana imposed by commitment to the Indiana Department of Correction under the above Cause number and Count are hereby completed.

Effective date of this final discharge is: (month, day, year)

06/21/2010

Approved by: (signature of Indiana Parole Board Chairman or Designee (Superintendent / Parole District Supervisor))	Date of signature (month, day, year)
	07/12/2010

DISTRIBUTION: Offender, Facility Packet, Central Office Packet, Committing Court

We work to
keep you working

IPLA
Professional Licensing Agency

Medical Licensing Board
402 W. Washington St. Room W072
Indianapolis, IN 46204
Tel : (317) 234-2060 Fax : (317) 233-4236

www.PLA.IN.gov
Governor Mitchell E. Daniels, Jr.

August 3, 2009

Van Johnson
Muncie Mission
1725 South Liberty
Muncie IN 47302

RE: 01037881A
Expiration Date: 06/30/1991

Dear Dr. Johnson:

Per your request, I have reviewed your revocation order and the one stipulation to reapplying is that you pay costs in the amount of $413.00 payable to Professional Licensing Agency.

Once you have paid the costs, you will need to complete a new application for licensure. I have enclosed an application and instructions. Once your application is complete you will be scheduled for a personal appearance before the Board.

If you have any questions, please feel free to contact the Medical Group at (317) 234-2060 or e-mail pla3@pla.IN.gov

Sincerely,

Jody Edens
Assistant Board Director

MEDICAL LICENSING BOARD OF INDIANA

www.PLA.IN.gov
Governor Mitchell E. Daniels, Jr.

Medical Licensing Board
402 W. Washington St. Room W072
Indianapolis, IN 46204
Tel : (317) 234-2060 Fax : (317) 233-4236

November 12, 2009

Van Johnson
111 Della Blues Street
Indianola MS 38751

RE: 01037881A
Expiration Date: 06/30/1991

Dear Dr. Johnson:

This is in response to your letter concerning your Indiana license.

I cannot say what your chances are of you obtaining a new Indiana license. You would be set for a hearing and it would be your responsibility to prove to the Board that you are fit to practice.

They would want to know what you have done to say current with practice issues and theories.

The $413.00 is not refundable as it was costs that you were ordered to pay in your revocation order.

If you decide you want to apply for a new license, you will need to complete the application on our website and supply all requested documents.

If you have any questions please feel free to contact me by email at   .in.gov

Sincerely,

Jody Edens
Jody Edens
Assistant Board Director

MEDICAL LICENSING BOARD OF INDIANA

DR. VAN JOHNSON, M.D.

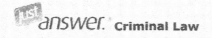 **Criminal Law**

Can a convicted felon practice medicine?

Sent to Criminal Law Experts 11/11/2009 at 10:30 AM

Can a convicted felon practice medicine?

Already Tried:
the conviction was in the state of Indiana. Doctor is open to practice in any state that will allow him to gain or renew his license. Had been licensed in Illiniois, Indiana, Kentucky.

Daffer58 (Online) -- 1 Accept / 1 Question

Status: Value: $15

1 Answer Accepted ⌄ ⎘ SHARE

Answer

11/11/2009 at 10:34 AM (4 minutes and 21 seconds later)

ACCEPTED ✓

Add Bonus

Yes it is possible based upon the discretion of the state board. You must be able to prove that the felony will not affect your ability to practice and that you have basically changed. That such a prior conviction is not indicative of future behavior. Obviously if the felony is connected with drugs or something concerning moral turpitude that will be harder to convince the board but it is possible.

If I have answered your question then please Accept the answer so I can receive credit for the response. Thank you and have a good day. NO ATTORNEY-CLIENT RELATIONSHIP EXISTS. PLEASE CONSULT A LAWYER IN YOUR STATE FOR LEGAL ADVICE

Daniel Solutions (Online)

✅ VERIFIED What's This?

100% Positive Feedback
126 Criminal Law Accepts

Criminal Defense Lawyer
over 20 years of legal and professor of law experience

Reply so we can help you better

Release Date:2007-02-13

- Styles -   B I U

Subject: Larry King Live

From: rosie king (orterness@yahoo.com)

To: vanjohnsonmd@yahoo.com;

Date: Friday, December 10, 2010 12:03 PM

Van,

Though I did not see or hear anything about you in the clip you are linked to Larry King Live on CNN. Search for GOOGLE then search from goolge for "Doctor Van Johnson Anderson Indiana murder" but remove the parenthesis. This search should lead to a clip from the Larry King show on the wrongfully convicted. There is a Book which chronicles " Tested" Wrongfully Convicted Felons. You can google chronicles " Tested" Wronfully Convicted Felons". There was also a hearing around October or November 2101 on a man called Cameron Todd Williams who was wrongfully put to death in Texas. See internet statement below.

1. **In case you missed it: Wrongfully convicted! – Larry King Live ... Oct 7, 2010 ... Dr. Van Johnson,M.D., October 11th, 2010 11:52 am ET ... who was also railroaded into prison in the state of indiana(the klan state). ...** *larrykinglive.blogs.cnn.com/.../in-case-you-missed-it-wrongfully-convicted/* - Cached

Legal lynching?

One of thousands of prisoners on lockdown in Indiana State Penitentiary; hot meal every two weeks. Inset: Dr. Van Johnson.

By Anthony D. Prince

CHICAGO—They say the truth is stranger than fiction, and the case of Dr. Van Johnson vs. the State of Indiana is proof.

On Saturday, January 23, the Universal Human Rights Organization of African People (UHRAP) met here to inform the public of the strange story of what happened in Anderson, Indiana.

It all began two years ago when Dr. Johnson, an African American psychiatrist, was forced to sue his employer, St. John's Hospital over the duties of his job. Johnson quit and set up his own practice, something that got quite a few people mad in an area known as "Klan country."

"He [Johnson] began to get threatening phone calls," says UHRAP Director Dr. Marguerite Price-Stamps. "They said the KKK was going to run him out of Indiana. A truck supposedly went out of control and slammed into his office. He began to fear he was being set up by the Anderson police and to show signs of stress, severe depression and nervousness."

By the time a white man, later identified as James Wagner, showed up unexpectedly and suspiciously on Dr. Johnson's porch on a Sunday night, the stage was set for something terrible to happen.

"Dr. Johnson states that he was paralyzed with fear," reads a UHRAP fact sheet. "When he went back to the bedroom the man was standing at the window. He got his gun."

What happened next, according to his supporters, was that the would-be intruder made a dash at the terrified Johnson whose gun accidentally discharged hitting Wagner in the chest. Johnson's own attempts to save the man's life failed, and he was still giving CPR to his victim when the police arrived. During questioning, says Price-Stamps, police wouldn't allow Johnson to see an attorney for hours and turned a tape recorder on and off in an attempt to twist Johnson's words.

Midway through the trial presiding Judge Fredrick Spencer referred to Supreme Court Justice Clarence Thomas as "an Oreo." Johnson's supporters say this remark was a clear indication of just what the young black doctor was up against. He was convicted of voluntary manslaughter and sentenced to 40 years in prison.

"Our whole thing," says Dr. Price-Stamps, Johnson's most ardent supporter, "is to bring this to the public. It's not just about Dr. Johnson. This could happen to anyone, regardless of the color of your skin."

To learn more about what can be done to free Dr. Van Johnson, contact: UHRAP at P.O. Box 53325, Chicago, Illinois 60653-0325. Phone 312-726-8426. Leave a message.

U.S. Department of Justice

Federal Bureau of Investigation

Washington, D. C. 20535-0001

June 18, 2014

Dr. Van Johnson
Post Office 19003
St. Louis, MO 63118

Dear Dr. Johnson:

This letter is in response to the correspondence you addressed to the FBI in which you allege your name has been wrongfully placed on a website listing sex offenders. You further allege this has led to verbal insults and harassment.

Please mail the specific details of your allegations to the FBI's St. Louis Division, located at 2222 Market Street, St. Louis, MO 63103, telephone number (314) 231-4324.

Sincerely yours,

Matthew W. Drake
Chief, Civil Rights Unit
Criminal Investigative Division

STATE OF INDIANA)
) SS :
COUNTY OF MADISON)

AFFIDAVIT TO REAFFIRM MOTION FOR MISTRIAL MADE BY PETITIONER/DEFENDANT AT VOIR DIRE

This affidavit concerns the events surrounding retrial of State of Indiana v. Johnson Cause No. 48C01-90006-CF-057. This trial was originally scheduled to begin on 6/4/96, but did not commence until 6/7/96. I (Petitioner/ Defendant) was transported in jail house clothing to the Madison Circuit Court from the Madison County Detention Center, in Anderson, Indiana. At the Courthouse defense counsel Montaque Oliver, Jr., then informed me that my trial was about to start. When we entered Courtroom, venire jury was already seated and Judge Spencer immediately brought the Court to session. Court asked defense counsel if he had anything to say. Counsel asked Defendant to stand up and proceeded to describe Blue Shirt and Pants as those normally worn by inmates in the County jail (made an Exhibit of defendants clothing).

I immediately made a floor motion for mistrial and reminded the Court that we previously objected to me being tried in jail clothes. It was also mentioned that my appearance in jail clothes would prejudice me in the eyes of the jury.

The Court blame defense counsel for my presence in jail clothes and denied motion for mistrial.

This motion for mistrial was not found in trial transcripts anywhere, and amounts to illegal expungment of evidence from the Court record.

22

Voir Dire proceedings are located in transcripts of evidence Volume IV of VII pages 424-654, in the Indiana Court of Appeals Cause No. 48A02-9610-CR-664.

Respectfully submitted,

Van Johnson, M.D.
Van Johnson, M.D., Affiant

AFFIRMATION

I, Van Johnson, M.D. do hereby affirm that the foregoing affidavit is true and correct to the best of my knowledge and belief.

Van Johnson, M.D.
Van Johnson, M.D. pro se

SUBSCRIBED AND SWORN TO before me, a Notary Public, in and for the State of Indiana, this _13_ day of July, 2007.

_____   _____
Notary Public Signature   Notary Public Printed Name

My Commission Expires :   County of Residence:
_01-29-09_   _LAKE_

23

DR. VAN JOHNSON, M.D.

WARNING **PARENTAL ADVISORY**

PROTECT YOUR CHILD FROM SEX OFFENDERS

Home | | New Search | Register | Member Login | Record Removal Inquiries

≥ return to search results ≤

Indiana Sex Offender Archive Record For: Van Johnson

Van Johnson
View photos:

Last known address:
1725 S Liberty St
Muncie   IN 47302

Gender: M
Age: 55
Height: 6 ft. 3 in.
Weight: 262
Build: Large
Race/Ethnicity: Black
Hair Color: Black
Eye Color: Brown

Offense: VOLUNTARY MANSLAUGHTER

Offense and Court Details		Supervision/Registration Details	
Statute:	[35-42-1-3]	Start Date:	2010-06-19
Conviction Date:	1996-07-15		
Release Date:	2009-06-18		

Criminal Records For Van Johnson

(For Background Checks about yourself or someone else click here)

- **YOUR SILENCE WILL NOT HELP THE NEXT VICTIM. Tell a Friend.**

To Alert Others About Van Johnson 's Sex Offender Record from Muncie in Just Click The Facebook Icon directly above the sex offenders record photo.

START A NEW SEX OFFENDER SEARCH

Dr. Van Johnson
P.O. Box 19003
St. Louis, MO 63118
zurdrax@hotmail.com
Cell phone 3142858905

Curriculum Vitae

EDUCATION:

Von Steuben Science Center College Preparatory	Chicago, IL
University of Illinois at Chicago Bachelor of Science Degree in Biology	Chicago, IL
Harvard University Health Careers Program--Fellowship	Cambridge, Mass
Rush Medical College Doctorate of Medicine	Chicago, IL
Mount Sinai Hospital Medical Center Pathology Internship	Chicago, IL
Jackson Park Hospital Family Practice Internship	Chicago, IL
Illinois State Psychiatric Institute Psychiatry Residency	Chicago, IL

1

Dr. Van Johnson
P.O. Box 19003
St. Louis, MO 63118
zurdrax@hotmail.com
Cell phone 3142858905

EXPERIENCE

Cumberland Hall Child/Adolescent Inpatient Psychiatric Hospital Medical Director	Hopkinsville, KY
Van Johnson Mental Health, Inc. Private Practice of Psychiatry	Anderson, IN
Mid-America Psychology Consulting Group Medical Director	Indianapolis, IN
Lawndale Mental Health Center Staff Psychiatrist	Chicago, IL
Englewood Mental Health Center Staff Psychiatrist	Chicago, IL
Bobby E. Wright Comprehensive Mental Health Center Staff Psychiatrist	Chicago, IL
Pontiac Correctional Facility Forensic Psychiatrist	Pontiac, IL
Joliet Correctional Facility Forensic Psychiatrist	Joliet, IL
Nile's Township Sheltered Workshop Consultant	Nile's Township, IL

2

Dr. Van Johnson
P.O. Box 19003
St. Louis, MO 63118
zurdrax@hotmail.com
Cell phone 3142858905

Organizations
Alpha Phi Alpha Fraternity, Inc. XI Lambda Chapter, Chicago, Illinois

Prince Hall, Free and Accepted Mason, Harmony Lodge #88; Chicago, Illinois

Honors:

Co-founder of the Health Careers Program, University of Illinois at Chicago

Student National Medical Association, Secretary of the chapter at Rush Medical College

Silver Medal, Chicago Park District Chess Championship

Bronze Harp, French horn Solo competition

The Author "Framed and Profiled"; the Legal Lynching of a Black Psychiatrist.

3

Supreme Court overturns psychiatrist's manslaughter conviction

By MIKE SMITH
Associated Press Writer

INDIANAPOLIS (AP) — The Indiana Supreme Court has reversed an Anderson psychiatrist's manslaughter conviction, saying testimony about a prior incident should not have been allowed at trial.

Van Johnson was convicted of voluntary manslaughter in the 1990 slaying of his newspaper carrier's father, James Wagner. The jury found Johnson innocent of murder but guilty of the lesser crime. He was sentenced to 30 years.

Johnson, who claimed the shooting was accidental, told police he shot Wagner after he noticed him darting from window to window at Johnson's apartment.

Neighbors and Wagner's family testified that Wagner was only collecting for newspaper delivery.

Johnson, whose blood-alcohol content tested at .22 percent five hours after the shooting, told police that when he opened his front door, Wagner rushed him. Drunkenness in Indiana is defined as .10 percent.

Johnson said he was from Chicago, and "in Chicago we shoot people like this," the ruling said.

The trial court should not have allowed testimony about an incident Johnson had two years prior to the shooting, the high court said.

In that incident, two management people from Johnson's apartment complex knocked on his door announcing they were from housekeeping. When nobody answered, one woman tried to use her passkey to open the door.

Johnson shouted "Don't come in, I will shoot." He then opened the door pointing a pistol at the woman. After seeing their identification and talking with them, he let them in so they could inspect his fire extinguisher.

Prosecutors said evidence of that incident was admissible because it showed Johnson's character.

The high court disagreed.

"We do not see how evidence of an incident in which the defendant confronted people other than and unrelated to the victim (Wagner) in this case and in which a shooting did not occur, makes it more likely either that Johnson knew that he was killing the victim or that the shooting was not an accident."

Attempts to reach Madison County prosecutors to see if they would attempt to retry the case without the inadmissible evidence were unsuccessful.

Montague Oliver Jr., Johnson's appeals attorney, did not immediately return a phone call seeking comment.

U H R A P

Universal Human Rights Organization of Afrikan People
P.O. Box 53325
Chicago, IL 60653-0325
(312) 726-8426

April, 10, 1993

Dr. William E. Marsh
Professor of Law.
c/o In. Univ. School of Law
Bloomington, In. 47405

Dr. Van Johnson, a former Chicago psychiatrist who was recently convicted of voluntary manslaughter in Anderson, Ind., was sentenced on August 19, 1992 to forty (40) years in prison.

Dr. Johnson's attorneys maintained throughout the trial that Dr. Johnson is innocent and that the shooting was accident and in self-defense.

Judge Fredrick Spencer, who presided over the case, while in full judicial attire, while on the bench in full view of everyone in the court room referred to Supreme Court Justice Clarence Thomas as an "oreo". Yet Judge Spencer was able to walk away with not even a slap on the wrist.

Noting that Dr. Johnson chose not to testify during the trial, when a witness for the defense who was a state trooper, on the stand tried to testify in reference to the conversation between her and Dr. Johnson two days prior to the shooting, Judge Spencer would not allow her testimony saying that it was hearsay. The prosecuting attorney, Lawler stated that if Dr. Johnson wanted to testify to his state of mind on the night of the incident then, he(Dr. Johnson), should get on the stand and testify in his own defense. Although the Judge admonished Lawler and ordered the statement strickened from the records, it was a negative statement and implanted in the minds of the jurors. If I were a juror, I would feel that maybe Dr. Johnson is hiding something if he's not willing to testify in his own behalf after hearing an inflammatory statement by the prosecuting attorney.

Also during deliberations, while deciding Dr. Johnson's fate, there was a evacuation of the jury due to a thunderstorm. There was a lot of confusion at one point. Lights in the courthouse went off and the alarms sounded. Eventually the jurors were led to the basement. Before that the spectators; and the family of the deceased were moved.

"Internationalizing the struggle of the descendants of former
Afrikan Slaves in North Amerikkka"

there also. There was conversation between the jurors and the family of
the deceased. The Defense Attorneys for Dr. Johnson called for a mistrial
that was denied by Judge Spencer. There were several occasions where the
the Defense Attorneys asked for mistrials only to be denied repeatedly
by Judge Spencer who, through out the trial abused his judicial discretion.

The deceased, James W. Wagner went to Dr. Johnsons home on the night
of June 10, 1990, allegedly under the pretext to collect newspaper money
from Dr. Johnson around nine o'clock p.m. (9:00 p.m.). Mr. Wagner did not
work for any newspaper company. He was an engineer at Delco-Remy Corp.

Enclosed is a fact sheet and articles relating to Dr. Johnson who
has no prior convictions nor any type of criminal background.

An appeal is in the works at the present but Dr. Johnson still re-
mains in prison and denied bail.

There was involvement of the KKK, in which the state of Indiana is
trying to supress.

We are seeking counsel for Dr. Johnson as well as asking for an in-
dependant investigation for Dr. Johnson to expose the case and all those
involved.

Thanking You in Advance

Marguerite Price

Marguerite Price, J.D.
Int.l. Director of U.H.R.A.P.
(Universal Human Rights
Organization of Afrikan People).